CAPTAIN JOHN SMITH
AND HIS BRAVE ADVENTURES

Captain John Smith and His Brave Adventures

R E Pritchard

HAUS BOOKS
London

Copyright © 2008 R E Pritchard

First published in Great Britain in 2008 by Haus Publishing,
26 Cadogan Court, Draycott Avenue, London SW3 3BX
www.hauspublishing.co.uk

The moral rights of the author have been asserted

A CIP catalogue record for this book is available from the British Library

ISBN 978-1-905791-25-5

Typeset in Garamond by MacGuru Ltd
info@macguru.org.uk

Printed and bound in India by International Print-O-Pac Limited
Cover illustration courtesy Topham PicturePoint

Contents

History is the memory of time,
the life of the dead,
and the happiness of the living.
Captain John Smith

Foreword

In thinking of the hero of this book, a modern, unheroic figure surprisingly comes to mind: A A Milne's Tigger, who Bounced before breakfast and all day, unstoppably. Certainly one of the most admirably bouncy – vigorous, resilient, unstoppable – Tiggers of the early 17th century was Captain John Smith. Christened in remotest Lincolnshire with a name so common as to be almost anonymous, he set out on what he called 'brave adventures' to make a name for himself, eventually becoming well known as a soldier, pirate, colonist leader and author. Little did he know – and he would not have been particularly pleased about it – that his name would forever be associated with that of a young Native American princess, Pocahontas.

What we know of his extraordinary career derives largely from his own writings, not remarkable for any false modesty, where his Tiggerish qualities of relentless optimism and energy – 'bounce' – are notable features. He began his career at 16, as a volunteer soldier in the Netherlands' war of independence from Spain. Later, fighting in the Balkans against the Ottoman Turks, he distinguished himself, being awarded the title of Captain; after killing three Turks in single combat, he was granted a coat of arms of three severed heads. Captured, he was enslaved, before killing his master and riding off into Russia. On his return, he went to Morocco, where he was briefly a pirate.

Back in England, he joined a colonisation venture to Virginia; surviving attempts to have him hanged for insubordination, he led expeditions into Indian territory. There he was captured and prepared for execution, until the intervention of the chief's young daughter, Pocahontas. A few years ago, Peggy Lee sang in 'Fever' how 'Captain Smith and Pocahontas / Had a very mad affair'. However, Pocahontas was only 11 and no Lolita, whilst Smith was as tough as old boots and somewhat puritanical. Later, he led more expeditions and was briefly President of the Council in Virginia, before a gunpowder explosion so injured him that he had to return to England.

There, after more unsuccessful expeditions, he briefly met Pocahontas and her English husband; he became a prolific writer, producing books about colonisation and seamanship, and his autobiography.

His accounts of his extraordinary adventures provoked many to doubt him, but patient, modern research has confirmed him as honest and reliable – if not absolutely objective. He writes not as a meticulous modern historian but as a Jacobean man of action, telling it as he saw it (and, curiously, in the third person; the relative absence of 'I' makes his writing seem less egocentric, if somewhat detached). Foreign names usually get mangled to correspond with what he heard, reported conversations, whilst retaining the gist of what was said, are tidied and polished, and sequences of events occasionally get muddled by memory. Only grammar-school educated like Shakespeare, he also incorporated other writers' material into his own, to fill things up and look better. For all that, whether as writer or fighter, he could be trusted. In this account of his life, 17th-century texts have been modernised as regards spelling and punctuation; interpolations in quoted texts are in square brackets. At this time, the English were still using the old, Julian calendar, but dates have been adjusted in accordance with the modern, Gregorian calendar. Here, Native Americans are referred to as Indians, as has been the practice from the time of Columbus, in Smith's time and until recently; no offence is intended.

John Smith was a remarkable man, in the great tradition of Elizabethan adventurers, brave, resourceful, intelligent and outspoken, with a vision of what America could become. His life reads like an adventure story, of battle, disasters, triumphs, of a refusal ever to give in. For his armorial bearings, he chose the motto, *Vincere est Vivere* – 'To Conquer is to Live'; Tigger would have translated it, 'Watch Me Bounce!'

1

Upon Brave Adventures

In January 1580, Cardinal Henry of Aviz, King of Portugal, died without a natural heir (as a celibate should) or confirmed successor. There was a brief war of succession, and Philip II, King of Spain, took the throne. In so doing, he united two vast colonial empires, that stretched from the Americas to the Netherlands and territories in Africa, India, China and the East Indies (in 1631, Smith wrote, 'The sun never sets in the Spanish dominions') – a huge superpower that lasted until 1640, when John of Braganza declared Portuguese independence. Despite its enormous wealth and power, it was not impregnable: in September that year, Francis Drake's *Golden Hind* came into Plymouth Sound after a three-year circumnavigation, laden with gold, silver and various exotica, including tomatoes, potatoes, pineapples and parrots, looted from Spanish and Portuguese territories around the world. Drake's cargo was valued conservatively (that is, excluding what he did not reveal to the Queen's accountants) at £600,000 (multiply by 25 or 30 to get a sense of the modern equivalent) – his investors made a profit of 4,700 per cent. Spain, its power, as well as resistance to and competition with it – and the profit to be made from robbing it – would dominate English thinking for years to come.

On 9 January of that same year, George Smith and his wife Alice (Rickards, of a Yorkshire family) presented their first-born son, John, for baptism at St Helen's Church (Helen, aptly as it turned out, being the patron saint of travellers), in Willoughby by Alford, in Lincolnshire. The village is in the east of the county, where the Lincolnshire wolds merge with the flat lands bordering the North Sea coast; to the west can be seen the towers of Lincoln Cathedral, and Tattershall Castle, the seat of the Earl of Lincoln. George, whose family originally came from Lancashire, farmed at Great Carlton, nearby, a little east of Louth, where he also had three plots of land. As a yeoman farmer, he was one of those whom William Harrison (in his *Description of England*, 1587) defines as owning land worth annually at least £2, who have 'a certain pre-eminence ... and commonly live wealthily [and] keep good houses ... for the most part farmers to gentlemen, [who] come to great wealth ... often setting their sons to the schools ... to make them by those means to become gentlemen'. Harrison also remarks, again aptly, 'these were they that in times past made all France afraid'. George did well: his will and inventory detail a substantial, five-room house, with oak beds, chairs and tables, painted cloth hangings on the walls, and brass and pewter dishes with other chattels valued at over £75. At his death he bequeathed two good horses to Sir Peregrine Bertie, Lord Willoughby de Eresby and Lord of the Manor of Willoughby (who had come into the title in 1580), from whom he rented a farm of over 100 acres, and with whom he seems to have been on good terms (to John's benefit).

In 1586, Lord Willoughby was sent to the Netherlands to join the Earl of Leicester fighting against the Spanish, succeeding Sir Philip Sidney as Governor of Bergen and becoming commander of the cavalry. The next year he was made commander of the English forces in the Netherlands, and successfully resisted the Duke of Parma's siege of Bergen, for which he was knighted. He seems to have acquired a reputation for courage, as indicated by 'The Ballad of Brave Lord Willoughby' (the date it mentions cannot be linked with any particular battle):

> 1. The fifteenth day of July
> With glistering spear and shield

A famous fight in Flanders
Was foughten in the field.
The most courageous officers
Were English captains three,
But the bravest man in battle
Was brave Lord Willoughby.

2. 'Stand to it, noble pikemen,
And look you round about,
And shoot you right, you bowmen,
And we will keep them out.
You musket and caliver men,
Do you prove true to me,
I'll be the foremost man in fight',
Says brave Lord Willoughby. ...

5. The sharp steel-pointed arrows
And bullets thick did fly,
Then did our valiant soldiers
Charge on most furiously:
Which made the Spaniards waver,
They thought it best to flee;
They feared the stout behaviour
Of brave Lord Willoughby. ...

The young John Smith would have been impressed by the reputation of his lord. A year later, 1588, there was more cause for excitement for a young boy, with the news of the approach of the great Spanish Armada: the whole country was alerted and aflame (literally, with warning beacons and watchtowers). Along the east coast of England, they prepared their 'Home Guard' to fight off Medina Sidonia's troops, as the Spanish fleet was driven northwards to its doom on the rocks of Scotland and Ireland. An adventurous boy would thrill to the thought of battle and glory.

The next year, Henri III of France was assassinated, leaving the crown to his Protestant cousin, Henri, King of Navarre. The year after, Willoughby was sent to help Henri, now Henri IV, against the Catholic resistance in northern France and Brittany, led by the Duke of Mercoeur, who in turn asked Philip of Spain for assistance. In 1593 Parliament called for renewed military efforts against Philip in Brittany, amid rumours that Drake (now Sir Francis) would go to sea again.

In that year, according to Smith's autobiographical *True Travels*, schoolboy John, 'his mind being even then set upon brave adventures', and stirred by all he had heard, 'sold his satchel, books and all he had, intending secretly to go to sea'. His education had begun at about the age of six or seven, at Queen Elizabeth's School in nearby Alford, under Francis Marbury, described later as 'a Puritan knave', who may well have influenced Smith's values. His ambitious father then sent him on to King Edward VI Grammar School in the larger town of Louth, some 12 miles away, that trained the sons of gentry for higher education. As a mere yeoman's son – rather short and red-haired, as well – John might have had difficulties. It is possible that here he met Lord Willoughby's elder son, Robert, three years his junior, though Robert was mostly taught by home tutors. The school had strict standards of behaviour: its seal bore a Latin motto (echoing Proverbs 13:24), to the effect that 'He that spares the rod hates his son', with a picture of a bearded teacher birching a boy. This was normal thinking and practice at the time; while never over-deferential to authority, John always valued discipline. The school day was long, from six in the morning until four or five in the afternoon. Teaching concentrated on reading and writing Latin, with some arithmetic and geography (deplorably utilitarian subjects – though Latin, as the lingua franca of Europe, could be useful abroad).

True Travels, written some 36 years later, is curiously muddled about the sequence of events, in that he writes that his father's dying when he was about 13 prevented him leaving, when in fact George did not die until 1596. His father, very much alive, kept him at school until 1595, when he was apprenticed to a merchant in King's Lynn, Thomas Sendall, a trader in wool and wine, known to Lord Willoughby, and 'the greatest merchant of all those parts', as town mayor and member of the Hanseatic League international trading organisation. This was a good position, with excellent prospects – and it did not suit young John at all. Practical man though he was later to become, as a romantic youth he found recording inventories and cargoes, fretting about tunnage and poundage, storage facilities and international exchange rates was not for him.

Then, in April 1596, George Smith did die. His will left John 'competent means', and his best bed and the farm to his wife, with the condition that should she marry again it would pass to John. Within a year, the farm, with seven more acres, was his. Such swift remarriages were common then, in a time of short life-expectancies. How teenager John reacted, we do not know (Hamlet was particularly resentful of 'wicked speed' and funeral baked meats served up cold at the wedding feast); he later 'killed off' his father before his time, he does not seem to have kept up with his mother (though he later remembered her, in Virginia), and his brother and sister might as well not have existed, for anything he tells us. As far as his family was concerned, Smith was indeed to be 'a self-made man'. With no interest in merchant-trading or farming, John was soon off, leaving the farm in the charge of guardians, who gave him 'out of his own estate, ten shillings to be rid of him' (the touch of resentment echoes down the years).

Smith's account is not clear at this point, but, like Shakespeare's Petruchio, driven by 'such winds as scatters young men through the world / To seek their fortunes farther than at home, / Where small experience grows', some time in 1596 or 1597 'he went with Captain Joseph Duxbury into the Low Countries' as a volunteer soldier of some kind, perhaps, as Ancient Pistol phrased it, trailing 'the puissant pike'. It was a rough, hard life: cannon, pike and musket might tear one open, the cavalry might trample one underfoot; often men had to sleep out in the open. Pay was supposed to be about eight pence a day, but it did not always arrive. There were supposed to be rations of salt beef, biscuit and beer, but in practice men were expected to provide for themselves. This usually meant stealing or buying from local inhabitants, or stealing from each other, as George Gascoigne, who had served there, wrote:

> No fear of laws can cause them for to care,
> But rob and reave, and steal without regard
> The father's coat, the brother's steed from stall:
> The dear friend's purse shall pickèd be for pence ...
> With 'Tant tra Tant', the camp is marching hence ...
> This cut-throat life, meseems, thou shouldst not like ...

In any case, John stuck it with his captain for about three years, though it is not clear when he left. A Captain Duxbury served under Sir Francis Vere (related by marriage to Lord Willoughby) at the siege and battle of Nieuport, 2 July 1600, when the Spanish forces were heavily defeated. Most of the alliance's losses were in Vere's contingent, and Duxbury may have been one of these.

Two years before, in 1598, Lord Willoughby had been made governor of the border town of Berwick-upon-Tweed; early next year his elder son, Robert Bertie (now Sir Robert, knighted at the age of 14 in the attack on Cadiz in 1596 – what it was to be a nobleman's son!) was in Orleans, and persuaded his father to let his younger brother, Peregrine, join him, with a tutor and two servants. Among his attendants, making a quick return from Lincolnshire, was their old acquaintance and former tenant's son, soldier John Smith. As it turned out, they could not keep him long, and soon 'sent him back again to his friends'. However, John was in no hurry to see Lincolnshire again, and instead went to Paris, where a distant friend of the Willoughbys, David Hume, sent him on his way with 'letters to his friends in Scotland to prefer [recommend] him to King James' – a court career seemed to beckon. The next step was to the port of Le Havre (where, he recalled, he had first learned soldiering with Captain Duxbury), where he got a boat to Enkhuizen, a Dutch fishing port. There he took ship bound for Leith, very near Edinburgh. Unfortunately, the stormy North Sea proved as friendly to him as to the

Armada, and he was wrecked on the shore of Lindisfarne Island, about a dozen miles from Berwick; after a brief recovery, he pressed on to Scotland, to deliver his letters. Here, he was treated kindly, so kindly that he was dissuaded from further pursuing this impossible idea of becoming a courtier: short, sturdy, blunt in manner, with modest education and less money, he was not going to appeal to James. Back to Lincolnshire he went, *reculer pour mieux sauter*: it was time to retreat, in order better to advance.

Apparently, he literally went into a retreat: 'within a short time glutted with too much company ... he retired himself into a little woody pasture, a good way from any town. Here by a fair brook he built a pavilion of boughs, where only in his clothes he lay.' He could have gone back to his farm, but only this absurdly romantic gesture would do – something straight out of popular chivalric stories of the hermit 'Knight of Low Degree'. Tom of Lincoln and Bevis of Hampton lived in fields and forests until their true nobility could be revealed, like Guy of Warwick, who fought in Flanders, Spain and Lombardy and against the Turks in Constantinople, before dying as a hermit. The chivalric dream was to shape much of young John's self-image and actions. Like a true knight, he even had a 'squire', a local lad, as an assistant; he recalls that his food was largely venison, which suggests that he was on Lord Willoughby's estate, with permission. In a practical version of the romance tradition he even studied 'magic' books – probably from Lord Willoughby's library – which were to prove useful later: a translation of Machiavelli's *The Art of War*, together with Vannocio Biringuccio's *Pirotechnia* (instructions on the military use of fireworks and explosives), and what he called 'Marcus Aurelius', actually a translation of Antonio de Guevara's *Diall of Princes, or Book of Marcus Aurelius* (advice on how to live a noble life, with warnings against getting too involved with women).

In the intervals of these studies he practised horsemanship; hearing of this, 'friends' (probably Lord Willoughby's family) arranged for him to go to Tattershall Castle, to practise in its tilt-yard with the Earl of Lincoln's Italian riding-master, Theodore Paleologue. Paleologue, a descendant of Constantine XI, the last Greek Emperor of the Byzantine Empire, overthrown by the Turks in 1453, proved to be an excellent riding-master, teaching the manage of lance and sword on horseback, as well teaching some Italian, and telling the impressionable 20-year-old of the depredations of, and the continuing wars against, the mighty Ottoman Empire in eastern Europe. Smith later wrote piously how he was distressed by Christians killing Christians in Europe; but here was a war – a Crusade – in which a chivalric Christian warrior, bent on 'brave adventures' and with a name to make, could honourably engage. A few years earlier, one of John's heroes, Sir Richard Grenville ('of *The Revenge*') had expressed John's feelings:

> Who seeks the way to win renown,
> Or flies with wings of high desire,
> Who seeks to wear the laurel crown,
> Or hath the mind that would aspire,
> Let him his native soil eschew,
> Let him go range, and seek anew ...
>
> Wherefore who list may live at home,
> To purchase fame I will go roam.

Once again he set off for the Netherlands, perhaps looking for Captain Duxbury. While there, perhaps uncertain as to his next move in the temporary lull in the fighting, he fell in with 'four French gallants', who told him that they too were going to join the armies of Rudolph II, King of Hungary and Holy Roman Emperor, in the war against the Turks. The plan was, to go to Brittany, to the Duchess of Mercoeur, whose husband, now reconciled to Henri IV, had been made General of the Imperial Army, and who would give them letters of introduction to the Duke.

Together they sailed off, avoiding the Spanish Netherlands, 'with such ill weather as winter affordeth', eventually arriving at St Valèry sur Somme, at the mouth of the river. Once there, the four men arranged with the ship's captain to have themselves rowed ashore with their luggage – and John's, promising to return for him. It appeared that the water was too rough for the boat to come back until the evening of the next day, when the master told him that they had gone on to Amiens, 'where they would stay his coming'. It was now obvious that young John had been tricked out of all he had, to the anger of his fellow passengers, who 'had like to have slain the master, and, had they known how, would have run away with the ship'.

One of the passengers, a soldier, told him that the ringleader was not 'Lord Depreau', as he claimed, but the son of a lawyer from Mortain in western Normandy, accompanied by three young citizens (that is, not gentlemen) whom Smith later called Courcelles, Lanelly and Montferrat (when he did not know or could not recall someone's name, he frequently applied some appropriate place-name).This soldier, whom Smith called Curzianvere, agreed to go after them with him. At last, they got to Mortain and 'Lord Depreau', but 'to small purpose': presumably Smith's goods were by now all gone. However, the local nobility heard of the young stranger's sorry plight, and looked after him and gave him a little money. With this he pushed on, now alone, to the Bay of St Michel, hoping to find a ship, but soon ran out of money and food, before being found, as in one of his romance stories, 'in a forest, near dead with grief and cold ... by a fair fountain under a tree' by a 'rich farmer'. Having recovered, he went on, until somewhere between Pontorson and Dinan, in a grove of trees, he came upon Courcelles.

Immediately they fought, but Smith had become a doughty swordsman; just in time, some local farmers came up and intervened, when Courcelles confessed what had happened. Now Smith was told of a young Protestant nobleman, the Comte de Plouër, residing nearby, who was not only an Anglophile but even had some connection with Lincolnshire. Once again, the young man was taken in, treated well and given some money, so that 'he was better refurnished than ever'. Young Smith was no polished charmer, but clearly had qualities – youthful enthusiasm and frankness? – that made people take to him and want to help him.

From Brittany he made his way south, probably on hired horses, reaching Marseilles early next year. Here he caught another ship, bound for Italy, that proved not very weatherly, being forced to shelter from storms in the lee of a small, barren island he thought was off Nice, in Savoy. Unfortunately, the passengers included 'a rabble of pilgrims of divers nations going to Rome', who saw Smith as a Protestant Jonah, and threw him overboard.

Fortunately, Smith could swim sufficiently well to get to the island and its atheistic goats. In the morning, he found two other ships sheltering; one turned out to be captained by a Breton, who took him on board, to travel with them. The ship then sailed south, past Corsica and Sardinia to Cape Bon on the north-eastern tip of Tunisia, then to Lampedusa and eventually to Alexandria, where it discharged its cargo. Now they went northwards to Iskanderun or Alexandretta, notoriously unhealthy, set in 'a great marsh full of bogs, fogs and frogs' (as an English traveller, Peter Mundy, described it), the port for the great trading centre of Aleppo. Here the French captain made a point of examining what ships were in the roads; the nature of his interest became apparent later. They then sailed past Greece, possibly sheltering briefly around Kallamata, near Cape Matapan, before calling in at Cephalonia and Corfu in the southern Adriatic (probably with a view to collecting wine, currants and spices).

Sailing through the Strait of Otranto, the captain sighted a Venetian argosy (the word derives from Ragusa, modern Dubrovnik, on the Adriatic coast). His approach was recognised as threatening, and was met with a cannon-shot that killed a member of the crew. This was sufficient for the Frenchman to counter-attack fiercely, first with a broadside, then with his stern cannon, then his other broadside and finally his chase, or bow, guns, 'till he gave them so many broadsides one after another, that the argosy's sails and tackling was so torn, she stood to her defence [could not sail away], and made shot for shot. Twice in one hour and a half the Breton boarded her, yet they cleared themselves; but, clapping her aboard again [coming close alongside], the argosy fired him [either deliberately or from flying cannon-wadding], which with much danger to them both was presently quenched.'

Having dealt with the damage, the Frenchman returned to the attack, and 'shot her so oft between wind and water, she was ready to sink'. Having lost some 20 men to the Frenchman's 15, and in a dangerous condition, the argosy surrendered. The French boarded again, some men working to stop her sinking, some to chain and guard the prisoners, and others to loot her. The cargo, wrote Smith, was 'wonderful': bales of silks, velvets, cloth of gold and tissue, and a variety of coins – 'piastres, chequins and sultanies, which is gold and silver'. It took them all day and night to unload their booty, before, 'tired with toil', they left, leaving behind 'as much good merchandise as would have filled their ship again'. This was much the kind of tax on profits that the merchants of Venice feared: 'ships are but boards, sailors but men; there be land-rats and water-rats, water-thieves and land-thieves – I mean pirates'. Having done their repairs, the part-time pirates headed west, slipping past some Spanish galleys near Messina, before arriving in Antibes, in Piedmont. Smith went on his way, rewarded for his share in piracy with 500 chequins 'and a little box God sent him [!] worth near as much more'.

The gifts of God and the French modified young Smith's plans somewhat, as he decided on a little touring, like any gentleman, 'to better his experience by the view of Italy'. As was his practice in his *True Travels*, he only listed the places he passed through, except for Siena, where, to his pleased surprise, he encountered the Bertie brothers (Robert now Lord Willoughby, on the recent death of his father), who were both 'cruelly wounded in a desperate fray, yet to their exceeding great honour'. He does not provide any details, though duelling over minuscule slights to honour was becoming more common among the aristocracy.

After a few days he went on, reaching Rome; like many stout English Protestants, he was fascinated by Roman Catholic beliefs and practices. Here, he relates, 'it was his chance to see Pope Clement the eight, with many Cardinals, creep up the holy stairs [the Scala Santa] which they say are those our Saviour Christ went up to Pontius Pilate, where, blood falling from his head, being pricked with his crown of thorns, the drops are marked with nails of steel; upon them none dare go but in that manner, saying so many Ave-Maries and Pater-Nosters, as is their devotion, and to kiss the nails of steel.'

More to the point, he also called upon 'the famous English Jesuit', Father Robert Parsons, notorious in England for having sneaked into the country in 1580 with Edmund Campion to encourage Catholic resistance there. It seemed that Smith was taking a great risk in visiting a Jesuit in Rome, for the Inquisition was vigorous in imprisoning and torturing any Protestants they could get their hands on. An Englishman named John Mole (or Molle), employed as tutor-companion to two young aristocrats, was arrested in 1638 and eventually died in prison, aged 80, after 30 years' imprisonment; others were tortured to death – a few even converted. On the other hand, Smith wanted to fight for the Catholic Emperor, in a holy war against the Turks: Parsons would have taken him in and provided the necessary directions and introductions. After a little more touring, Smith reached Venice, where he found a ship that sailed, by a roundabout route trading with Ragusa and the Dalmatian coast, to Capo d'Istria, directly across the Gulf of Venice where he had started. From there, at last, John was on his way.

To Conquer is to Live

Whenhen Smith set off to fight the Turks in Hungary, he began by seeking out the Duc de Mercoeur and Father Parsons, knowing that the war was not simply a matter of Christian West against Muslim East, but overwhelmingly a Catholic enterprise. That, however, was not the half of it: these wars were more of a bloody dogfight, involving Catholics, Protestants, Muslims, Hungarians, Transylvanians, Germans, Poles, Turks, Tartars, visiting Italians and Frenchmen, wandering brigands and desperate peasants. A modern historian describes it as 'a brew in a witch's cauldron. No one knows any longer who is who and what is what ... Pillage, rape, the despoiling of orphans and widows, destruction of all values ... Once, sometimes twice a year Turkish Tartars lay waste this morsel of a country [Transylvania], pillaging and burning where they pass, destroying most of all its human substance. They drive the population away in chain gangs, to the slave markets of distant Crimea.' To understand something of what happened to Smith in Hungary and Transylvania, some outline knowledge of Balkan history is needed.

In 1453 the Turkish Sultan destroyed the remains of the Eastern Roman Empire, and soon the great Ottoman Empire came to extend northwards throughout Eastern Europe into Poland and to the gates of Vienna. Central Hungary had been under Turkish domination since 1541, with the fertile little province of Transylvania to the east as a semi-independent protectorate, with Zsigmond Bathory as prince since 1581, while the north and west were under the aegis of the (German) Habsburg, Rudolph II, King of Hungary and, more important, Holy Roman Emperor. His prime concern was to regain control of Hungary and Transylvania for Roman Catholicism and the Empire, itself a loose federation of smaller states stretching from Flanders to parts of Poland and Hungary. Rudolph looked to Catholic Europe for assistance, while suppressing the Calvinist, Lutheran and Unitarian populace. Rudolph had been declared insane in 1598 (for what difference that made), whilst Zsigmond was described by a contemporary as *'fluctuantibis undis instabilior'* – less stable than the fluctuating waves. His elder cousin, Elizabeth, was to become notorious for trying to preserve her beauty by bathing in the blood of freshly murdered young women – reportedly, the remains of some 650 were later found in her castle (Cahtice, in modern Slovakia). In the intervals of striving to establish his rule (the Protestant people preferred him to German Catholic or Turkish Muslim rule) Zsigmond nevertheless abdicated four times; at different times he sought to be a king or a cardinal; married to Rudolph's first cousin, the marriage was not consummated, his impotence being attributed, by a Vatican commission, to witchcraft. The Scottish traveller, William Lithgow, who was in the area in those years, wrote that the Hungarians 'have ever been thievish, treacherous and false, so that one brother will hardly trust another, which infidelity amongst themselves and distracted, deceitful governors was the chiefest cause of their overthrow and subjection under infidels. And so have corrupt councillors and insolent princes been the ruin of their own kingdoms' (not that Lithgow thought highly of any foreigners). It is hardly surprising that the whole bewildering history of the time is characterised by constantly changing loyalties, betrayal and murder.

In 1596 Zsigmond, with Mihail Vitas (Michael the Brave), Prince of Wallachia, defeated the Turkish Grand Vizier Pasha in a battle on the Danube, only to be defeated himself the year after. The next year, he abdicated for the first time, leaving Transylvania to the care of his wife's cousin, the Emperor, but returned within a few months. There followed some unsuccessful peace negotiations, and in 1599 he abdicated again, leaving Transylvania to his cousin, Cardinal Andrew Bathory, who was then overthrown (beheaded by Protestant peasants who chopped off his finger for the cardinal's ring) by Michael, who was then recognised by Rudolph as Imperial Governor of Transylvania. However, the people resisted him, so Rudolph sent his general, Giorgio Basta, to put down the resistance, which he did, brutally, while also driving out Michael, before leaving. Zsigmond then collected an army and returned early in 1601. Michael managed to reconcile himself with Rudolph, and he and Basta joined forces to drive out Zsigmond (into neighbouring Moldavia), before Basta had Michael murdered.

Meanwhile, the Turks had captured the key strategic fortress of Nagykanizsa in 1600. Rudolph and the Pope now appealed to Christendom for help; Christendom was generally busy elsewhere, but some Catholic princes and noblemen responded, including some Gonzagas from Italy and the Duc de Mercoeur. There were some Protestants, but they were generally not especially welcome. In August 1601 the Imperial headquarters were set up in Graz in Austria, and Rudolph grouped his forces into three: one army under Ferraste Gonzaga with Basta as his general, one commanded by Ferdinand Gonzaga, and one overseen by Rudolph's brother, the Archduke Matthias, with the Duc de Mercoeur as his general.

John Smith now arrived, presumably with a letter of introduction from Father Parsons to an Irish Jesuit and English Catholic, who in turn introduced him to 'Lord Ebersbaught' (as Smith called him: probably Sigismund, Freiherr von Ebiswald). This led him to the 'Generall of the Artillerie, Baron Kissel', Hanns Jacob Khissl, Baron von Kaltenbrunn, in charge of the ordnance, explosives and munitions generally. Smith's contacts had all been Catholic, but as a Protestant he had to be moved on to a Protestant Hungarian regiment, under the 'Earl of Meldritch', Count Modrusch.

As part of the campaign to regain Nagykanizsa, Modrusch's men were sent to relieve Ebiswald's forces, now besieged by the Turks in

'Olumpagh' (Lower Limbach, modern Lendava). This was Smith's first action in these wars, and he made the most of it. His reading in his 'little woody pasture' in Lincolnshire had included Biringuccio's *Pirotechnia*, with instructions on secret signalling lights. Smith now got to Khissl and told him that he had instructed Ebiswald in a particular technique. The method was to divide the alphabet, A to L, M to Z: in the first half, a single light would be shown in sequence up to the desired letter – thus, E would have five lights, one after another; in the second half, two paired lights would be counted up – thus, O would be indicated by 2, 2, 2. The end of a word would be marked by three lights together. The system was ponderous, but adequate. Smith was given guides to a hill-top where he set up three flaming torches as an initial signal, which was soon answered from inside the town. He then sent his message, very concisely, to the effect: 'On Thursday at night I will charge on the East, at the alarum, sally you'; this was agreed.

Khissl was still uncertain of his success, but Smith and his guides pointed out that the Turkish forces were divided by the river, and so unable to reinforce each other; and Smith came up with another device. This was to light up, at the time of the attack, two or three thousand pieces of tow tied together, to look like the 'matches' of matchlock muskets being lit in preparation for an attack. This was done; the Turks rushed out in force to counter this presumed attack, in the wrong direction, while Khissl's soldiers got in from another direction. 'It was not long ere Ebersbaught was pell-mell with them in their trenches, in which distracted confusion a third part of the Turks that besieged that side towards Knousbruck were slain; many of the rest drowned, but all fled. The other part of the army was so busied to resist the false fires, that Khissl before the morning put two thousand good soldiers in the town.' The Turks raised the siege and withdrew, and Khissl moved on to Körmend, where Smith was rewarded and promoted to Captain of 250 horsemen, under Count Modrusch.

Mercoeur then moved on, in September 1601, to besiege the city of Stuhlweissenburg (also known as Alba Regia or Alba Regalis in Latin, the former coronation and burial place of Hungarian kings), where the Turks initially inflicted heavy losses. This was a walled, fortified city surrounded by marshes and, on patches of higher ground, walled suburban villages. However, to the west, the suburb of Sziget was relatively defenceless, because of the marshland and river, which is where Mercoeur decided to make his main attack. Camped on the north-east, he set up a relentless cannonade to hold the Turks' attention, and Smith was again able to use his pyrotechnics, particularly his 'fiery dragons'. This was a device generally known as 'Greek Fire', that worked rather like modern napalm, sticking and burning. Taking 40 or 50 earthenware pots filled with gunpowder, pitch, brimstone and turpentine, stuck about with musket-balls and covered with flammable cloth, he had them ignited and slung, rather like mortar-shells, over the walls into the city. 'At midnight upon the alarum, it was a fearful sight to see the short flaming course of their flight in the air, but presently, after their fall, the lamentable noise of the miserable slaughtered Turks was most wonderful to hear.' Meanwhile, Mercoeur's second-in-command, the Graf von Russworm, with a thousand men each carrying a float made of sedge and branches, splashed and waded through the marsh and mud, to attack and rapidly occupy Sziget. The Turks were now closed in. A few days later, on 20 September, Mercoeur's artillery breached the walls; fierce hand-to-hand fighting ensued, destroying large parts of the city (as an officer in Vietnam said, 'we had to destroy the place in order to liberate it'), before the Pasha, to save his own life, surrendered to Modrusch in person.

Nevertheless, the Turks had not given up here, and sent a large force to regain the city; Mercoeur, having garrisoned Alba Regalis, met them on the way with a smaller force. There were violent, deadly skirmishes: 'Here Earl Modrusch was so environed amongst those half-circular regiments of Turks, they supposed him their prisoner, and his regiment lost; but his two most courageous friends, Vahan [Von Wagenberg] and Culnitz [Kollnitz], made such a passage amongst them that it was a terror to see how horse and man lay sprawling and tumbling, some one way, some another on the ground... . Captain Smith had his horse slain under him, and himself sore wounded; but he was not long unmounted, for there was choice enough of horses that wanted masters.' The Turks then besieged Alba Regalis, but were defeated at a battle nearby, where Smith also fought, under the command of Kollnitz.

Meanwhile, that autumn, Zsigmond, 'beyond all belief of men', as Smith wrote, was back again in southern Transylvania, with popular support and now with some Turkish backing, and with some degree of success. This was too much for Rudolph, who promoted Basta to commander-in-chief of the Imperial Army in Transylvania, with orders to get rid of Zsigmond by whatever means necessary. For the winter of 1601, Mercoeur regrouped his armies, sending one under Russworm to Nagykanizsa, his own into winter quarters to garrison the Danube, and the third, under Modrusch, to Transylvania with instructions to help Basta. He himself then left, intending to recruit more soldiers in France, but died on the way, in Nuremburg.

Modrusch and his men arrived at Basta's headquarters in late February or early March. Mercoeur's death had dispirited his men; at this point Basta also left, with some of the Imperial Army. Even more important was Basta's brutal and cruel treatment of Transylvanians and Hungarians, with pillaging, looting, murder and rape on a large scale. Whole cities were given over to the soldiers as free for looting, farm buildings, storehouses and crops were destroyed, and desperate starvation and even cannibalism ensued. While Hungarians were fighting for Rudolph in Hungary, his men were destroying Hungarians in Transylvania.

During the winter, Basta and Zsigmond had been in secret negotiations, and arranged a temporary truce on 13 February; one of the terms of this was that Zsigmond was given liberty to drive out of the country Basta's haiduks ('hydukes', as Smith spelled the word). These haiduks were mercenaries, robbers and brigands, some originally driven out of Hungary to wander as cattle-herders, but now largely Tartars and renegade Turks, who made up an unreliable and uncontrollable part of Basta's forces, and were chiefly responsible for most of the atrocities. The death of Mercoeur, the disengagement of Basta and the horrors carried out by his haiduks all led Modrusch to persuade his men not to assist Basta, but instead to follow him in assisting Zsigmond.

Their services having been promptly and gratefully accepted, Modrusch's forces then hunted the haiduks in 'the Land of Zarkam' (Zarand, west of Alba Julia). They camped somewhere on what Smith later, not remembering or not even having known the proper name, called 'the plains of Regall'. This name derived from a (his?) mistranslation of the Latin text of Smith's grant of arms, taken to suggest that there was a town called Regal – there was not – when the army was in fact proceeding 'ad urbem regalem', that is, 'towards the royal city', which would be Alba-Julia (in modern western Romania), where Transylvanian princes had formerly had their residences.

After a bitter winter and hard marches, as Smith reports, 'the earth no sooner put on her green habit than the Earl overspread her with his armed troops', making 'many incursions among the rocky mountains', clearing out minor fortresses held by 'some Turks, some Tartars, but most Bandittoes, renegades and such like' (haiduks), before reaching Alba Julia, a 'city not only of men and fortifications strong of itself, but so environed with mountains that made the passages so difficult, that in all these wars no attempt had been made upon it to any purpose'.

The strength of the position meant that Modrusch could not take it with his 8,000 men. He began with a stratagem to seize a position of vantage in a narrow valley between high mountains: here he sent a Colonel Veltus (as Smith calls him) to gather all the cattle roaming in the plain and, early in the morning, drive them past a small fort in the valley. The defenders came out to bring them in, but were cut off by Veltus's troops lying hidden in ambush, who then seized the fort.

It still took Modrusch six days of hard work to get his artillery through the rocky defiles and in front of the city, which the Turks had freshly strengthened. In fact, before his men could even pitch their tents, the Turks had sallied forth in such strength that a fierce hour-long battle ensued (with sword, pike and musket), with heavy losses on both sides, until Modrusch could get his cannon in position and force a Turkish withdrawal. The next day reinforcements arrived, consisting of 9,000 footsoldiers and 26 more cannon, under the command of Moses Székely, the general. The Turks' position was very strong; it would require a prolonged, organised siege to remove them. Earthworks had to be prepared, and great ramps set up, to get the heavy artillery in position to bombard the city's defences.

While this heavy labour was going on – over a month, at a deliberate pace – with only minor skirmishes to enliven the boredom, the Turks sent out derisive messages, mocking the delay. At last, a challenge was issued, to any captain in the Christian army: 'That to delight the ladies, who did long to see some court-like pastime, the Lord Turbashaw [a bashi, or Turkish captain] did defy any captain that had the command of a company, who durst combat with him for his head.' In other words, a formal duel on horseback and in armour, to the death, the winner to behead the loser, and keep the head as a trophy. Smith makes it sound like something out of his chivalric romances, with 'ladies' (probably camp-followers and 'comfort women') and 'court-like pastime', but apparently such combats were in reality not uncommon in these wars. The poet-dramatist, Ben Jonson, boasted to Drummond of Hawthornden how 'in his service in the Low Countries [probably in 1591] he had in face of both the camps killed an enemy [in single combat] and taken *opima spolia* [rich spoils – armour] from him'; his biographer remarks how 'the day labourer became the hero of a chivalric passage of arms'.

Naturally, there was some lively discussion of this, as to who was have the honour of being the Christian champion. 'It was decided by lot'; it comes as no surprise that, somehow, Smith – never backward in coming forward – won. He describes the action quite well.

'Truce being made for that time, the rampiers [city ramparts] all beset with fair dames and men in arms, the Christians in battalio [battle array], Turbashaw with a noise of hautboes [oboes, reedy wind instruments] entered the field well mounted and armed. On his shoulders were fixed a pair of great wings, compacted of eagles' feathers within a ridge of silver, richly garnished with gold and precious stones, a janissary [one of the Turks' crack infantrymen] before him bearing his lance, on each side another leading his horse; where long he stayed not ere Smith, with a noise of trumpets, only a page bearing his lance, passing by him with a courteous salute, took his ground with such good success that, at the sound of the charge, [with his lance] he passed the Turk through the sight of his beaver [the face guard of his helmet], face, head and all, that he fell dead to the ground; where alighting and unbracing his helmet [Smith] cut off his head, and the Turks took his body; and so returned without any hurt at all.'

Smith presented the head to General Székely, who 'kindly accepted it', while the Christian army cheered. However, a friend of the vanquished Turk, named by Smith 'Grualgo', now 'enraged with madness', directed a challenge specifically to Smith, to regain his friend's head or lose his own, with a bonus prize of the loser's horse and armour for the winner; it was agreed for the next day. Once again, spectators assembled, the trumpets sounded and the horses charged; this time, both lances were shattered by the violent impact, and the Turk was nearly unhorsed. Now it was pistols, at close range; Grualgo's shot struck Smith on his breast-plate, while the Turk was wounded in his left arm (presumably holding the reins). The horse panicked and reared, and the Turk, unable now to control it, was thrown to the ground, bruised and stunned, unable to defend himself. Smith leapt down, seized his man as he lay there, and hacked off his head. Afterwards, he kept the horse and armour, according to the agreement, but the body, in its rich clothing, was returned to the Turks; presumably, Székely added the head to his collection.

The siege resumed its slow progress, the gun ramps rising remorselessly; 'every day the Turks made some sallies, but few skirmishes would they endure to any purpose'. At last Smith, 'with so many incontradictable persuading reasons [nag, nag]' got permission to issue his own challenge (usual terms and conditions applied). The challenge was promptly accepted, by one rejoicing in the name, as Smith thought, of Bonny Mulgro: not a show-off or distraught friend, but a serious fighter. Smith gives a fairly detailed account of what was clearly a ferocious encounter:

'The next day both the champions entering the field as before, each discharging their pistol (having no lances but such martial weapons as the defendant appointed) [the Turk having seen what Smith could do with a lance], no hurt was done. Their battle-axes were next, whose piercing bills [hooked blades] made sometime the one, sometime the other to have scarce sense to keep their saddles, specially the Christian received such a blow that he lost his battle-axe, and failed not much to have fallen after it, whereat the supposing conquering Turk had a great shout from the ramparts. The Turk prosecuted his advantage to the uttermost of his power [a phrase concealing what must have been a storm of the most violent batterings]; yet the other, what by the readiness of his horse, and his judgement and dexterity in such a business, beyond all men's expectations, by God's assistance [and thanks to Palaeologue's lessons back in Lincolnshire], not only avoided the Turk's violence, but, having drawn his falchion [curved broadsword], pierced the Turk so under the culets [overlapping armour plates protecting the lower back] through back and body, that although he alighted from his horse, he stood not long ere he lost his head, as the rest had done.'

The Turkish ladies were disappointed; Smith, by the sound of it, would have been very battered and bruised; but the Christian soldiers, understandably delighted, led him with a huge, noisy guard of honour and three horses, each with a Turk's head impaled and dripping on a lance, to the pavilion of the General, who rose to the occasion, embracing him and giving him a horse richly equipped, and a scimitar and belt worth 300 ducats, while Modrusch in turn promoted him to Sergeant Major (equivalent to a major, a title he never used).

At last the great timber-framed earth ramps were completed, 50 or 60 feet high, with 26 heavy cannon aimed at and over the city walls; the great, smashing cannonade began, pounding into the walls, hour after hour, day after day. Within 15 days two great breaches in the walls had been made; savage and desperate fighting took place in the rubble-filled gaps, choked with smoke and dust, 'that day was made darksome night [but for] the light that proceeded from the murdering muskets and peace-making cannon' (a rare venture by Smith into fancy prose). The 'slothful' Turkish governor had retreated to a hilltop castle, out of harm's way, but Székely commanded a general assault up the slope before the walls. This proved exceptionally difficult, with nearly half the attackers killed or thrown back by the logs, bags of gunpowder and stones hurled down the hill. Nevertheless, with great determination they forced their way up, to encounter the equally determined enemy with 'push of pike' and hand to hand fighting, but without success; but then Modrusch reinforced them with fresh regiments and the Turks were at last overwhelmed, and driven into the castle. Here they raised a flag of truce, and asked for terms of surrender.

However, Modrusch 'remembering his father's death' (Smith believed he was a Transylvanian, betrayed by Turks) declined terms, and battered the castle with all his artillery, until he seized it the next day; there, amid the dust and ruins, 'all he found could bear arms he put to the sword, and set their heads upon stakes round about the walls, in the same manner they had used the Christians when they took it.' War is not gallant duelling, but slaughter and revenge.

Székely, having plundered the Turks' camp, it 'having been for a long time an impregnable den of thieves', reconstructed the defences and put in a strong holding garrison, before setting off with his main force down the river valley, sacking towns and villages along the way – to the victor the spoils – until he came to Weissenberg, and the palace of Prince Zsigmond. The Prince there reviewed the conquering army, and was presented with 32 captured battle ensigns and some 2,000 prisoners, 'most women and children' (we are not told what he did with them; slavery would have been their best hope). A service of 'thanks to Almighty God in triumph of these victories' followed. He was then informed, among other reports, of Smith's earlier battlefield achievements. For these, and for his three duels fought by the laws of single combat, Smith was awarded armorial bearings – a coat of arms – to be worn on his shield: a device of three Turks' heads. Zsigmond also awarded him a medallion of himself set in gold, and an annual pension of 300 ducats. John Smith, yeoman's son from Lincolnshire, was now 'an English gentleman', in Europe at least – but not, as he was to find, in England.

Meanwhile (this history is all 'meanwhile') Basta had returned with fresh troops, and an offer from Rudolph to Zsigmond that he could hardly refuse: either retirement to his promised fiefdoms and a handsome pension, or all-out war. Transylvanian loyalists at court were not happy at the prospect of being abandoned to the mercies of Catholic Habsburg rule. In an attempt to ensure that Zsigmond did not accept, his general, Moses Székely, the victor of 'Regall', ambushed Basta's army as it approached Alba Julia, on 2 July 1602; Székely was defeated, and fled to Temesvar (modern Timisoara). Zsigmond immediately sent word to Basta disclaiming all knowledge and responsibility for this action; on 8 July, they met; and on 26 July Zsigmond abdicated for the last time, leaving Transylvania, in Smith's words, 'the very spectacle of desolation; their fruits and fields overgrown with weeds, their churches and battered palaces and best buildings, so for fear, hid with moss and ivy.'

In Wallachia, the war went on. The Emperor's chosen Voivode (prince) of Wallachia, Radul Serban, was being opposed by the Turks' chosen voivode; having got rid of their first choice he was now being threatened by the brother, Jeremia Movila, with a large army of Turks, Tartars and Moldavians. Basta had now acquired Zsigmond's former troops (including those of Modrusch); doubtful of their loyalty, and preferring to preserve his own men, he sent off Modrusch to deal with Movila. Movila in turn called for support from Chancellor Zamoyski of Poland (under his control) and from the Tartar Khan of Crimea, Ghazi II Geray (also known, unpromisingly, as Bora, 'the drunken camel'), who would eventually provide a large and fearsome army. *En route* to confront Zamoyski, Radul's army proceeded along the River Olt by Hermannstadt and 'the Red Tower Pass', camping at 'Reza'; Movila's men sat down nearby, awaiting the Tartar reinforcements.

Minor sorties and engagements ensued, with the usual savagery: Radul beheaded his prisoners and threw back the heads, Movila flayed alive his and hung the heads and skins on stakes. Radul then tried to

draw Movila into battle before the Tartars arrived, by a tactic of advanc-
ing ('burning and spoiling all where he came') and then withdrawing
as if in retreat. The Turks fell into the trap and pursued, a fierce battle
ensuing. In the battle, Modrusch's horse was killed under him. 'Thus
being joined in this bloody massacre, that there was scarce ground to
stand upon but upon the dead carcasses, which in less than an hour were
so mingled, as if each regiment had singled out other.... . It was reported
that Jeremia was also slain, but it was not so, but fled with the remainder
of his army to Moldavia, leaving five and twenty thousand dead in the
field, of both armies. And thus Radul was seated again in his sovereignty,
and Wallachia became subject to the Emperor.'

Modrusch was then sent off with 11,000 men to deal with reported
Tartar outriders and stragglers, but instead bumped into Movila in
ambush at Langenau with 14–15,000 men – and with Geray on the way
with a reported force of 30,000 Tartars. Modrusch beat a hasty retreat
toward the relative security of the Red Tower Pass. On the way, however,
they were hindered by constant attacks from skirmishers. One night,
they had to struggle through a wood, hacking down trees to clear their
way and to block their pursuers'. In the dim, misty early morning light
they came upon some 2,000 pillagers (many of them haiduks reverting
to their cattle-herding past) with 200–300 horses and cattle. Most of
these they also hacked down; the surviving prisoners told them where
Movila was nearby, his Tartars close behind. Modrusch knew he had to
get away quickly, and Smith came up with another 'pretty stratagem':
this was to fill 200–300 explosive cases with wildfire, like that he had
used before, put them on lances, and charge the enemy in the night.
This terrified the horses and unnerved the men, causing a stampede, and
Modrusch and his men got through with negligible losses, hurrying as
best they could towards the pass.

But within a few miles, Ghazi's Tartars, 30–40,000 strong, caught up
with them: 'they must either fight, or be cut in pieces flying'.

As Smith wrote later, 'Here Busca [his version of Basta] and the
Emperor had their desire', recognising the inveterate hostility of their

supposed allies. 'The sun no sooner displayed his beams than the Tartar his colours, where at midday he stayed awhile to see the passage of a tyrannical and treacherous imposture, till the earth did blush with the blood of honesty, that the sun for shame did hide himself from so monstrous sight of a cowardly calamity.'

For a moment, the 'pride, pomp and circumstance of glorious war' (in Othello's phrase) caught his imagination. 'It was a most brave sight to see the banners and ensigns streaming in the air, the glittering of armour, the variety of colours, the motion of plumes, the forests of lances and the thickness of shorter weapons', but it could not last – 'the silent expedition of the bloody blast from the murdering ordnance, whose roaring voice is not so soon heard as felt by the aimed-at object, which made among them [the Tartars] a most lamentable slaughter.'

Modrusch had quickly arranged his 11,000 as best he could: in front, he set a screen of sharp stakes and a triple row of pikes, with footsoldiers interspersed in pits like foxholes, to help in a delaying action. The Tartars charged 'with a general shout, all their ensigns displaying, drums beating, trumpets and oboes sounding'; two cavalry regiments counter-attacked and forced a temporary withdrawal, before a second assault, 'darkening the skies with their flights of numberless arrows', though held off for over an hour, at last forced the Christians back behind their stakes.

The Turks charged for victory – into the stakes and concealed foot soldiers: 'it was a wonder to see how horse and man came to the ground among the stakes, whose disordered troops were there so mangled that the Christians with a loud shout cried, Victoria!' Five or six cannon added to the slaughter. Nevertheless, realising that he was being pushed back and could not hold out much longer against overwhelming numbers, Modrusch gathered his men to make a dash for the river gorge behind him. For half an hour, it seemed to succeed, but the main force of Tartars in their thousands, with two regiments of Turks and Turkish janissaries (crack soldiers) caught them, and overwhelmed them.

As night fell, Modrusch and about 1,400 cavalry swam the river; some drowned (few people could swim then, especially when battle-weary and burdened with armour); those who stayed behind, fought, fought in vain, and were almost all killed. 'And in this bloody field, near 30,000 lay; some headless, armless and legless, all cut and mangled; where breathing their last, they gave this knowledge to the world, that for the lives of so few, the Crim-Tartar never paid dearer.' Smith lists the names of dead leaders, and eight Englishmen; only two other Englishmen survived, Ensign Thomas Carleton and Sergeant Edward Robinson (who somehow got back to England and later contributed commendatory verses to two of his books).

At dawn, the pillagers and scavengers, knives at the ready, picked over the remains, chasing off the greedy crows, finishing off the hopelessly wounded, stripping the bodies of anything valuable, dragging out any wounded that might still be useful. 'Smith, among the slaughtered dead bodies and many a gasping soul, with toil and wounds lay groaning amongst the rest, till being found by the pillagers he was able to live, and perceiving by his armour [perhaps Grualgo's, won in single combat] and habit [they stripped off the armour] his ransom might be better to them than his death, they led him prisoner with many others.'

His part in this vicious, futile war was, though he might not yet have realised it, over. Later, he gave the date as 18 November 1602.

Dangerous Service

O nce Smith was sufficiently recovered from his wounds he was marched off to a slave market, in a town he later thought was Axiopolis (near modern Cernavoda, in Romania). Here the prisoners were 'all sold for slaves, like beasts in a market-place, where every merchant, viewing their limbs and wounds, caused other slaves to struggle with them, to try their strength'. Smith would probably have been known to have been an officer, and therefore potentially valuable, for ransom, or useful as an enforced soldier or janissary. In the market he was bought by one he called 'Bashaw Bogall', who 'sent him forthwith to Adrinopolis [modern Edirne], so for Constantinople to his fair mistress for a slave. By twenty and twenty chained by the necks, they marched in file to this great city [about 150 miles to the south]'. The English traveller, Fynes Moryson, records how slave 'merchants ... buying their captives, lead them bound to one another in chains, forcing the sick and weak with whips to march as fast as the rest, or else cut their throats if they be not able to go, and at night when they are brought into a stable and might hope for rest, then they suffer hunger, the men are scourged with whips, the women and boys are so prostituted to lust, as their miserable outcries yield a woeful sound to all that are near them'.

Constantinople, the capital of the Ottoman Empire – not that he probably saw much of it – was one of the great world cities, an urban monster of well over 400,000 inhabitants (George Sandys, another English traveller, estimated a population of 700,000, half Turkish and half Jews and Greek Christians), with 2,000 mosques, including Santa Sophia, and 300 public baths, as well as the Sultan's great palaces and, on Wednesdays, a great slave market. This dealt mostly, wrote William Lithgow, in 'Hungarians, Transylvanians, Carinthians, Istrians and Dalmatians', as well as whatever the corsair raiders brought in from the length and breadth of the Mediterranean (and even farther abroad: in 1630 they captured six ships from Bristol, and in 1645 raided Fowey in Cornwall, enslaving 240 inhabitants). Here 'they were delivered to their several masters, and he to the young Charatza Tragabigzanda.' This name – better Trabigzanda – was simply Greek for 'girl from Trebizond' (an ancient Byzantine city on the south-east coast of the Black Sea); possibly she was herself Greek in origin. In 1614, sailing along the coast of New England, he named a point of land (now Cape Ann) Trabigzanda.

This young lady took an interest in her new present, especially as her admirer, the Bashaw, had written to the effect that this was 'a Bohemian Lord conquered by his [own] hand, as he had many others, which ere long he would present her, whose ransoms should adorn her with the glory of his conquests'. Taking her opportunity when she was allowed out (George Sandys reported that Turkish women 'never stir forth but to pray at the graves and to the public bannias [baths]'), she questioned him, wherever he was kept – they both had some Italian, and some of her friends had smatterings of English, French and Dutch – and soon discovered that he was an Englishman, no Lord, but 'only by his adventures made a captain'. She 'took (as it seemed) much compassion on him'.

Smith states that she had no practical use for him, and so, 'lest her mother should sell him', she now decided to send him on to her brother, who was in charge of a *timar* or military fiefdom on the far side of the Black Sea, telling him that Smith was 'there but to sojourn to learn the language, and what it was to be a Turk, till time made her master of herself'. Clearly he was to be made fit for service in the Ottoman Empire (many captives and former slaves rose to high positions), possibly by becoming a Muslim, and so available for promotion (perhaps as a senior janissary, to which he would be suited), and even for marriage when she was old enough.

So off he went, under escort, back north the way he had come, to Varna, a port on the west coast of the Black Sea; marched along under restraint, he noted what he could see, 'the towns with their short towers, and a most plain, fertile and delicate country'. Then it was by boat eastwards across the Black Sea, past the Crimea and through the 'Strait of Niger', the Kerch Strait, into the Sea of Azov with its muddy shoals and low islands, up to the 'river Bruapo', presumably the River Don. Sailing up this for six or seven days, 'he saw four or five seeming strong castles of stone and battlements about them, but arriving at Cambia [a name invented years later when writing his book – it is unlikely that his guards troubled to keep their prisoner well informed] he was, according to their custom, well used.' Here, by the river, itself half a mile wide, was a large castle with thick walls and a moat, and a town of low, flat houses, that kept 'the barbarous countries about it in subjection and admiration'. At last, after two more days' journeying, he was brought to 'Nalbrits', an ancient city named Nalbars or Naubaris, where Charatza's brother, the timariot, 'then was resident, in a great vast stony castle with many great courts about it, environed with high stone walls, where was quartered their arms, when they first subjected those countries, which only live to labour for those tyrannical Turks'.

The brother was now shown Charatza's letter regarding Smith's training, which he promptly put into force (the right word). What Smith did not understand was that his treatment was standard for those who were to be 'broken in' for service. Samuel Purchas recorded of such training, 'when one ... hath run through all the orders ... he is, without all question, the most mortified and patient man in the world. For the blows which they suffer, and the fastings which are commanded them for every small fault, is a thing of great admiration.' Whatever Smith had expected, he was shocked when 'within an hour after his arrival, [the timariot] caused his dragoman to strip him naked, and shave his head and beard so bare as his hand, a great ring of iron with a long stalk bowed like a sickle riveted about his neck, and a coat made of ulgries' hair [coarse wool from an 'argali' sheep] guarded [belted] about with a piece of undressed skin.' There were other Christian slaves there, with 'near an hundred forzados [galley slaves] of Turks and Moors, and he being the last was slave of slaves to them all.' It was, he wrote, a life that 'a dog could hardly have lived to endure ... no more regarded than a beast.'

While the timariot and his men fed well on meat, rice and coffee, the slaves got left-overs of boiled couscous and scraps of animal entrails. Smith thought that his only hope 'to be delivered from this thraldom' was 'the love of Trabigzanda', whilst long-serving slaves assured him hopelessly that there was no chance of escape from their guards and this back end of the world; but, as Smith added, 'God beyond man's expectation or imagination helpeth his servants, when they least think of help.'

At harvest time (this would be in late summer 1603) he was sent as thresher to a grange some distance from the timariot's house. During one inspection visit, the timariot, coming alone, for some reason 'took occasion so to beat, spurn and revile him, that, forgetting all reason, [Smith] beat out the Timar's brains with his threshing bat (for they have no flails)'. Whether he had indeed been provoked or, what seems more likely, had simply been awaiting his opportunity (and later did not want to admit to something like murder), Smith was now committed to prompt action. Swiftly he put on the timariot's clothes, hid the body under the straw, filled his knapsack, closed the barn doors, mounted the timariot's horse and galloped off, away into the empty landscape, 'at all adventure'.

For two or three days he wandered, completely at a loss, taking care not to be seen by anyone. At last, either by chance or remembering what some other slave had told him, he came upon 'the great way or Castragan, as they call it' – the great caravan trade-route from Poland to Astrakhan (in Russian, 'k Astrakhanu' – 'towards Astrakhan') and the east. At junctions along the way were signposts, marked with symbols: the track leading to Turkish Crimea had an Islamic half-moon (not the way to go), that toward Georgia, a black man with white spots, that towards

China and the east showed the sun, and, best of all, the track towards Muscovy, a cross – and Smith went that way. For sixteen days he rode on northwards through the empty steppes (hungrily, one imagines), always fearful of recognition as an escaped slave and recapture, and, if returned to 'Nalbrits', a very horrible death (the Turks were quite inventive in such matters). At last he arrived at a Muscovite garrison he later called Aecopolis (possibly Valuiki), about 200 miles northwards. Wherever this lonely outpost was, its governor had Smith's irons removed, and treated him well, so that 'he thought himself new risen from death', while his wife 'the good Lady Callamata largely supplied all his wants'. There has been speculation as to the lady's name (though Salamata was apparently a Don Cossack name) and also about the last four words.

Here he recovered for a while; at last a convoy set out towards Moscow, taking letters and reports, and Smith along with it, with a certificate or report from the governor. At 'Caragnaw' (Chernava, 20 miles south-west of Yelets, itself 200 miles south of Moscow) the governor also treated him kindly and gave him a letter of safe-conduct, which took him on, first to Dankov, then westward to Bryansk, Novhorod-Siversky, in northern Ukraine, and 200 miles on to Rechytsa, in southern Belarus. He lists the names of the towns he passed through in his own spelling, based on what he heard and remembered, and helped later by contemporary maps (which often spelled the names differently). As a young, escaped Christian officer, he was treated with great generosity; as he wrote, 'in all his life he seldom met with more respect, mirth, content and entertainment; and not any governor where he came but gave him somewhat as a present, besides his charges [expenses], seeing themselves as subject to the like calamity'. All this, in very poor 'continually foraged countries ... rather to be pitied than envied; and it is a wonder any should make wars for them [one remembers J-L Borges' remark about two bald men fighting for a comb]'. The villages consisted of only a few log cabins, the towns defended by log palisades and ditches, with a few small pieces of ordnance and bows and arrows. As for the roads, or tracks, 'you shall find pavements over bogs, only of young fir trees laid cross one over another, for two or three hours' journey, or as the passage requires, and yet in two days' travel you shall scarce see six habitations'. He pushed down southwards and, at last, at long last, he got back among old friends in Transylvania, at Hermannstadt (modern Sibiu).

Resting here, he would have been brought up to date about the latest developments in that unhappy country and at home – the death of old Queen Elizabeth – before 'glutted with content and near drowned with joy', he set off again, to find Zsigmond, get his pension and arms confirmed, and even perhaps 'rejoice himself in his native country'. His roundabout route took him through 'high Hungaria' (Slovakia), Tokay, Kosice, then through the mountains to Prague, where he learned that Zsigmond was now in Leipzig, somewhat of a Protestant island in the Catholic Holy Roman Empire (like nearby Wittenberg, where Hamlet was supposed to have been a student). No doubt to his great pleasure, his old commander Modrusch was also there, and may have helped him to an audience with Zsigmond. It proved worth all the effort getting there: in lieu of the annual pension, he was given 1,500 gold ducats and a laisser-passer, 'intimating the service he had done, and the honours he had received'. This invaluable document described him, in Latin, as 'an English gentleman' and a former Captain, authorised to wear three Turks' heads on his shield, and requested all authorities to permit him unhindered passage through their lands. This document, dated 9 December 1603, was later accepted and approved by the Garter King of Arms, who in 1625 granted Smith the coat of arms it authorised.

With his new money and passport, there was no need to hurry home, and Smith now set off on further travels, in effect as a tourist – unless he was seeking employment as a soldier for one of the German princes. He did not bother to transcribe any touristic travelogue of the relatively familiar country he travelled through, merely listing names, from Dresden to Augsburg to Frankfurt, west to Strasburg and Nancy in Lorraine. He then crossed France (Paris, Orleans) to Nantes in Brittany (presumably calling in at Plouër), where he took ship for Bilbao.

This was a most remarkable course of action: few English Protestants dared enter the land of the Spanish Inquisition, and those that did frequently had cause to regret it. The Scot William Lithgow was horrifically tortured in Malaga as an English Protestant spy, from November 1620 almost to Easter 1621, when he was starved, beaten, submitted to the rack and water torture, crushed and hanged by the toes, leaving him with broken bones and crippled. Perhaps Smith felt safe now that King James had replaced Queen Elizabeth and Philip III had succeeded Philip II, and preliminary peace discussions had begun; perhaps Zsigmond's laisser-passer provided security. In any event, he crossed the hot, hilly peninsula safely ('a barren, ill-manured soil,' wrote Lithgow, 'so desertous that in the very heart of Spain I have gone eighteen leagues, two days' journey, unseeing house or village ... miserable travelling, hard lodging and poor'); once again, he merely listed place-names on his direct route south to Cadiz and San Lucar.

'Being then satisfied with Europe and Asia, understanding of the wars in Barbary [the north African states from Morocco eastwards] he went from Gibraltar to Ceuta and Tangier, thence to Safi [a major port, some 300-odd miles south-west on the Atlantic coast].' Here, while on the look-out for possible employment in the impending wars, he fell in with the captain of a French man-of-war (as Smith called it) loitering there, and together, with a party of twelve, they went back inland, ostensibly 'to see the ancient monuments of that large renowned city [Tangier]'. His account, based on this visit, is amplified by borrowings, this time from writings by Leo Africanus, as translated in Purchas. Tangier, situated on the choke point of the busy trade route from Italy and the Levant through to western Europe, was a city of strategic importance. Smith touches on the former grandeur of the city, and writes for himself, elegiacally, of the 'famous universities, which are now but stables for fowls and beasts, and the houses in most parts lie tumbled one above another; the walls of earth are with the great fresh floods washed to the ground, nor is there any village in it but tents for strangers, Berbers and Moors ... dung-hills, pigeon-houses, shrubs and bushes ... lamentable ruins and sad desolation.'

He then went on to provide an account of the internecine wars of the time, between 'Mully Hamet' (Mulai Ahmed) and his sons: 'the wars being ended and Befferes [Abu Faris] possessed of Morocco and his father's treasure, a new bruit [rumour] arose amongst them, that Muly Sidon [Mulai Zidan] was raising an army against him, who after took his brother Befferes prisoner; but by reason of the uncertainty, and the perfidious, treacherous, bloody murders rather than war amongst these perfidious, barbarous Moors, Smith returned with Merham [the French captain, so called by Smith] and the rest to Safi, and so aboard his ship, to try some other conclusions at sea.' Perhaps Smith had had enough experience of betrayal and counter-betrayal; perhaps there was no opportunity for real soldiering; one might guess at what he had in mind by 'other conclusions at sea'.

In any case, Smith provides a story of how the French captain, moored in the open roadstead (Safi had no proper harbour), invited Smith and some others on board for dinner, 'till it was too late to go on shore, so that necessity constrained them to stay aboard'. By midnight, a fierce storm blew up, forcing them to slip cable and anchor, and put to sea, 'spooning before the wind till they were driven to the Canaries'. After it calmed, 'they accommodated themselves, hoping this strange accident might yet produce some good event'. Smith presents himself as driven by wind and circumstance – but he took all his money and papers with him when he went out to dinner. Clearly the Frenchman was a corsair or privateer: Morocco, like the other Barbary states, was notorious as a haven for corsairs (whether African, Turkish or European) paying taxes to the local rulers on their profits made from the sale of captured merchandise and the sailors and passengers, sold on in their thousands in the slave markets of north Africa and Turkey. In his *True Travels*, Smith was to write of pirates, how James's peace policy meant that he had no use for 'men of war', some of whom went off to make a living as pirates. He mentions how one Peter 'Easton got so much as made himself a marquis in Savoy, and [John] Ward [who captured a Venetian treasure-ship, and whom Lithgow later met in retirement in Tangier] lived like a Bashaw in Barbary.' Manifestly, there was money to be made, but most of the European corsairs wasted theirs: 'all they got they basely consumed it amongst Jews, Turks, Moors and whores' – not Smith's style. No doubt, Smith's happy memories of his own earlier attack on a Venetian argosy would have encouraged him on this course of action. Soon Merham and he had taken two or three small cargo ships, before they learned of five Dutch warships nearby (the Europeans were trying to suppress the corsairs), and quickly sailed away to Bojador [Boujdour], about 150 miles away on the coast of Africa.

Once there, Merham steered southwards towards a cape called Cabo de Não (Nouadhibou), where they encountered two ships sailing together. Smith's account seems worth quoting at length (C S Forester or Patrick O'Brian might not have been ashamed of it).

'Merham, intending to know what they were, hailed them; very civilly they danced their topsails, and desired the man of war to come aboard them and take what they would, for they were but two poor distressed Biscayers. But Merham, the old fox, seeing himself in the lion's paws, sprang his luff [tacked closer to the wind], the other tacked after him, and came close up to his nether quarter, gave his broadside, and so luffed up to windward. The vice-admiral [smaller, secondary vessel] did the like, and at the next bout, the admiral with a noise of trumpets and all his ordnance, murderers [small, light cannon, often used to clear decks when boarding] and muskets, boarded him on his broad side; the other in like manner on his lee quarter, that it was so dark, there was little light but fire and smoke. Long he stayed not, before he fell off, leaving four or five of his men sprawling over the grating [open trellis hatchway cover, often set up during close fights].

'After they had battered Merham about an hour, they boarded him again as before, and threw four kedges or grapnels in iron chains, then sheering off: they thought so to have torn down the grating, but the admiral's yard [the cross-spar supporting a sail] was so entangled in their [Merham's] shrouds [rigging], Merham had time to discharge two cross-bar shot amongst them [Smith's definition, in *A Sea Grammar* (1627) :

"A round shot with a long spike of iron cast with it, as if it did go through the midst of it."], and divers bolts of iron made for that purpose, against his bow, that made such a breach he feared they both should have sunk for company. So that the Spaniard was as yare [quick, adept] in slipping his chained grapnels as Merham was in cutting the tackling [that] kept fast their yards in his shrouds.'

Having drifted apart, they kept firing at each other intermittently from noon until six at night; Merham then sailed off towards Morocco, but with the others in close pursuit all night. Early in the morning, the two ships closed in, firing with their forward chasers, then their broadsides and even bringing their stern guns to bear, closing in even more, to musket-shot range. After an hour of this barrage they called on Merham to surrender: 'Merham drank to them, and so discharged his quarter pieces [stern cannon]'. They came in and boarded again, and some even climbed up the rigging to try to unsling the mainsail, but were brought down by musket-fire and knife-work. 'About the round-house [the *Sea Grammar* again: "The Master's cabin, called the roundhouse ... is the utmost of all, built on the after part of the quarter deck"], the Spaniards were so pestered, that they were forced to the great cabin and blew it up.' The struggle grew even more fierce and destructive: in the forecastle also the grating got blown up, 'with a great many of Spaniards more', which forced them to get off. Merham then got his weary men to put out the fires with water and wet sail-cloth, 'the Spaniards still playing upon him with all the shot they could. The open places [smashed open by cannon-shot and fire] they covered with old sails, and prepared themselves to fight to the last man.' In the face of such a determined, implacable foe, and after such a savage conflict, there was not anything else to do.

The Spaniards then put out a flag of truce, ostensibly for a parley, but Merham suspected a trap and took the opportunity to fire back, very effectively. 'Thus they spent the next afternoon, and half the night.' Came the pre-dawn light, and the Spanish ships had gone, having either lost them in the night, or given it up as a bad job and futile waste of men and ammunition. As Merham supervised the repairs, he found the ship had received 149 great shot, with 27 men killed and 16 wounded (cannon or musket-shot, burns, flying splinters and hand-to-hand fighting). 'A wounded Spaniard they kept alive' (interesting phrasing) said that the Spanish had lost 100 men, and had feared being sunk.

'Then reaccommodating their sails, they sailed for Santa Cruz [Madeira, where they would have undertaken further repairs], Cape Ghir and Mogador [Agadir?], till they came again to Safi.' Here Smith said farewell to Merham and his surviving shipmates, and also to the corsair life, that had proved less appealing than expected. Later, in *A Sea Grammar*, he wrote, 'I confess, the charging upon trenches, and the entrances of a breach in a rampart are attempts as desperate as a man would think could be performed, but he that hath tried himself as oft in the entering a resisting ship as I have done, both them and the other, he would surely confess there is no such dangerous service ashore, as a resolved, resolute fight at sea.'

At last he set off for England. He does not report his route back; he could have slogged back again through Spain and France, but very probably went by sea, which would have been quicker, cheaper and safer (pirates permitting). The old sailors' song, 'Farewell and adieu to you fair Spanish ladies' indicates the normal passage up-Channel:

> – from Ushant to Scilly 'tis thirty-five leagues.
> The first land we made it is callèd the Dodman,
> Next Rame Head off Plymouth, Start, Portland and Wight,
> And we sailèd by Beachy, Fairlight and Dungeness,
> Until we brought to by the South Foreland Light.

Home was the sailor, home from sea, and still with 'one thousand ducats in his purse', and looking for action.

4

Go West, Young Man

The English were slow off the mark in the race for America. In 1488, Bartholomew Columbus, brother of Christopher, approached Henry VII with a proposal for a fleet to sail west to reach the spice islands of the East Indies, and was turned down by that economical monarch. However, in 1497 Henry approved an exploratory voyage commanded by John Cabot, who reached Newfoundland, before disappearing at sea on a second venture in 1498.

Not until Henry's granddaughter, Elizabeth, was on the throne was there another serious effort, when Sir Humphrey Gilbert returned from conquests and plantation in Ireland with the idea of setting up comparable plantations in the New World. He persuaded the Queen to grant a licence for 'such remote, heathen and barbarous lands, countries and territories not actually possessed of any Christian prince', and set off with five ships in 1578. Only one got far beyond English waters, and that only to the Cape Verde islands; its captain was Gilbert's half-brother, the young Walter Ralegh. Undaunted, Gilbert set about organising a second attempt, despite his own financial difficulties – at one point, he complained that he had had to sell the clothes off his wife's back. To fund the expedition, he promised investors enormous tracts of American land in 'Norumbega' (what would become New England); interest was further aroused by a map he had, that showed the interior of North America crossed by great, wide waterways, surely providing access to the Pacific and East Indies. (It would be many years before Europeans realised the size of America: as late as 1612, when Dudley Digges calculated *The Circumference of the Earth*, he estimated that a mere 300 miles separated Virginia from Drake's New Albion, that is, California.) At first the Queen would not give him permission to sail himself, observing that he was 'a man noted of not good hap [luck] by sea', but eventually relented.

In June 1583 Gilbert sailed with five ships; one, owned by Ralegh and carrying important supplies, soon had to turn back because of illness among the crew. After seven weeks the rest arrived at St John's, Newfoundland – 'hideous rocks and mountains, bare of trees and void of any green herb' – which he formally 'took possession of ... in the right of the crown of England', before sailing south. Things continued to go badly: one ship had to go back, laden with people sick of dysentery and the whole enterprise, another ran aground and was wrecked, with the loss of 100 lives. Eventually he agreed to return also, and, to demonstrate that this was not for lack of personal courage, ostentatiously embarked in the smaller remaining ship, the *Squirrel*. As they neared the Azores, they 'met with very foul weather, and terrible seas breaking short and high, pyramid-wise ... Men which all their lives had occupied the sea never saw more outrageous seas.' The *Squirrel* began to founder. As the others came close, they saw Gilbert on deck, 'sitting abaft with a book in his hand'; he called out, 'We are as near to heaven by sea as by land'. That night, he and all his crew were drowned. Not good hap.

Next year, Ralegh took over Gilbert's patent on American colonisation, and sent out reconnaissance ships, piloted by a Portuguese navigator, one Simon Fernandes. Sailing via the Canary Islands and the West Indies, in July 'they felt a most delicate sweet smell', though they saw no land', and eventually arrived at a series of long, narrow islands, to be called the Outer Banks, along the North Carolina coast; behind these was the shallow, stormy Pamlico Sound. They anchored on the island of Hatteras, finding fruitful soil, abundant wild life and friendly – if semi-naked – natives. The captain, Arthur Barlowe, reported that the local

king was named Wingina and the country was known as Winganda-
coa (later it transpired that this meant only, 'You have nice clothes').
The king's name sounded like a word familiar to Ralegh and Elizabeth,
and the American coastal area between Newfoundland and Spanish
Florida became known as Virginia, after the Virgin Queen. The natives
were so friendly that two, Manteo and Wanchese, were later brought
back to England. Wingina suggested that the nearby island of Roanoke
might do for a settlement – he had people living there – and this, they
reported, would indeed make a suitable base for a colony, out of sight of
any passing Spanish ships.

On their return, Ralegh went for assistance to the Revd Richard
Hakluyt, a great enthusiast and collector of reports on exploration (in
1582 he published his first collection, *Divers Voyages as Touching the
Discoverie of America*). Hakluyt's report to the Queen, *A Discourse of
Western Planting* (i.e., colonising) helped persuade Elizabeth to approve
her favourite (now Sir) Walter Ralegh's patent and proposal – this time
to be funded partly by privateering attacks on the Spanish. Perhaps
remembering Gilbert's fate, she refused Ralegh permission to go, so he
recruited a cousin, the fiery-tempered Sir Richard Grenville, as commander of the group, which set sail in April 1583.

Two of the party are worth particular mention: one was John White,
who had worked as official artist on an earlier expedition for the North-
West Passage, the other was the brilliant mathematician Thomas Harriot,
who worked with Manteo and Wanchese to compile an alphabet and
dictionary of Algonquian, the natives' language. A selection of engrav-
ings of White's water-colours of Native American life was published in
1590 by Theodor De Bry, along with Harriot's *A Briefe and True Report
of the New Found Land of Virginia* (which failed to confirm Barlowe's
belief in the natives' innocence and simplicity); remarkably, Harriot's
book was the first to promote the health-giving properties of what was
to become the financial mainstay of Virginia – tobacco.

After a brief but violent encounter with the natives, Grenville got
Wingina's agreement for the settlement on Roanoke, and sailed off in

August, leaving some 108 colonists under the command of Ralph Lane, a veteran of the Irish wars. Unfortunately, before the expedition even reached Roanoke, their supply ship, the *Tiger*, had gone aground on the Outer Banks, with the loss of almost all their food supplies and seeds, which meant that the colonists, with limited survival skills, would be on very short rations and increasingly dependent on Wingina's goodwill in trading for food. As time went on, relations deteriorated, as Lane's aggression alienated the natives; fearing an attack, Lane got his retaliation in first, attacking the chief's village, killing many and returning with Wingina's head.

In the meantime, Grenville had returned to England, boasting of the establishment of the colony but warning of its depleted resources. Ralegh had intended a supply ship should promptly follow the first fleet, but the sharply increased hostility with Spain prevented this. Nevertheless, early in June 1586 a fleet commanded by Sir Francis Drake arrived off the Outer Banks. Drake had been raiding the Spanish in the Caribbean, but, hearing of a Spanish scheme against the colony, sailed north. Lane told him of the colonists' difficult situation, and asked that the whole colony be transferred northwards to the more promising situation in the Chesapeake Bay area. Drake agreed, but a terrible storm, probably a hurricane, blew up, causing the loss of the proposed transport ship, and it became apparent that the only course was to pack up and return to England.

Despite the bad reports that the colonists gave, Ralegh was determined to persist with his scheme for a 'City of Ralegh' in Virginia, and three more ships and 150 colonists set off for Chesapeake Bay in May 1587. John White, accompanied by his pregnant daughter, was to be the governor; Manteo was to become a Lord of Roanoke; and Simon Fernandes was to command the fleet. However, on reaching Roanoke, Fernandes refused to go any further north (he had some Caribbean privateering in mind), and, despite White's helpless fury, that was where they had to stay. Once again, there was trouble with the natives; White's granddaughter, Virginia Dare, was born; and there were renewed anxieties about food supplies. Ralegh's relief ship was supposed to go to

Chesapeake Bay, and might not look for them here. At last it was agreed
that White should return to England in the smaller of Fernandes' ships,
to ensure 'the better and sooner obtaining of supplies'. Those remaining
were never seen again by any European.

In November 1587, England was caught up in naval preparations
against the forthcoming Spanish Armada, and not one ship could be
spared for White. It was not until April that he was loaned two little pin-
naces – which, with their all-important supplies, were promptly seized
by French privateers. Then, in July 1588, came the great, doomed Armada
itself.

Not until March 1590 could White try again, in a five-ship fleet
of Ralegh's that was more intent on attacking Spanish treasure ships;
however, in August, two ships arrived off Roanoke Island. Here they
saw two fires, not signal fires as they hoped, but bush fires. When they
landed, after a fierce gale that drowned seven men, they called and sang
out, but heard only the wind sighing in the trees. In the silent remains
of the wooden fort, the houses had been taken down and the furnish-
ings removed. Buried chests containing valuables, including books and
pictures by White, had been dug up and ransacked. On a tree they found
carved the letters CRO – the beginning of the name of a nearby island,
Croatoan. White had arranged that if the colonists left, they would
carve the name of their destination on a tree; if they left in danger or
trouble, they should carve a cross by the name. Now, on a gatepost,
they found 'five foot from the ground, in fair capital letters, was graven
CROATOAN without any cross or sign of distress'. Puzzled as to why
the colonists should have gone there, they still had hope, as Croatoan
was 'the place where Manteo was born, and the savages of the island our
friends'; but when they tried to get there, the wind and sea got up again
alarmingly, driving the ships towards the shore. The captain decided
it was too dangerous, and to go back again to the Caribbean, returning to Croatoan in the spring. White reluctantly agreed, but even this
proved impossible, as they fell in with and joined a privateering fleet
commanded by Sir John Hawkins. Across the Atlantic and northward

they went, landing at Plymouth in October 1590. White gave up hope of ever seeing again his daughter, granddaughter or his colony, and died in Ireland three years later.

When Ralegh went to Guiana in unsuccessful search of El Dorado in 1595, he tried to get to Roanoke but was driven off by bad weather; three more expeditions were sent out in 1599, without any success. Interest in the colonisation of America seemed to have lapsed. Then, in 1600, the first edition of Richard Hakluyt's great *Principall Navigations, Voiages, Traffiques and Discoveries of the English Nation* was published, pointing out, amongst much else, that Cortez had captured Montezuma's empire, urging English emulation, and provoking fresh interest in trade and exploration. In the same year, the East India Company was founded; Hakluyt was made secretary and a very wealthy merchant, Thomas Smith, made a governor. The company's early financial success encouraged its governors to consider an American venture – largely financed by the Earl of Southampton, Shakespeare's patron – and in March 1602 they sent out Captain Bartholomew Gosnold, a kinsman of Thomas Smith. Gosnold sailed directly across to Maine, then past land that he named Cape Cod and an island he named after his dead daughter, Martha's Vineyard. He then briefly established friendly relations with the natives in northern Virginia, bringing back cedar wood, furs and sassafras, a kind of laurel with reddish-brown wood, believed to be useful against syphilis. Clearly, trade was possible, and could be profitable.

In 1604, another exploratory expedition had reached Virginia, under Captain George Waymouth, who met friendly natives – and kidnapped five of them. On his return to Plymouth, the Governor of Plymouth Fort, Sir Ferdinando Gorges, took them, keeping three and sending two up to London, where they caused a great sensation by demonstrating their skill at paddling a canoe on the Thames: they were paid four pence and five pence. Particularly interested were Robert Cecil, King James's adviser, and the Lord Chief Justice, Sir John Popham ('a huge, heavy, ugly man', according to John Aubrey, who 'lived like a hog' and eventually 'died by excess'). Popham had long been concerned about the unemployed poor, considering them parasitic, idle rogues and vagabonds, and had even drafted a bill to have them transported abroad; now, it seemed, America might do very well as a dumping-ground. Interest in colonisation and the import/export business was growing: cloth could be exported to semi-naked savages, and furs, fish, timber and gold – especially gold – imported. In 1605, in Ben Jonson's comedy, *Eastward Ho*, the sea captain Seagull claimed not only that the Roanoke colonists were still alive – 'They have married with the Indians, and make 'em bring forth as beautiful faces as any we have in England' – but also, more excitingly (though cribbing from Thomas More's *Utopia*), that in Virginia

> gold is more plentiful there than copper is with us ... Why, man, all their dripping pans and their chamber pots are pure gold; and all the chains with which they chain up their streets are massy gold; all the prisoners they take are fettered in gold ...

The country, he said, was as pleasant

> as ever the sun shined on, temperate and full of sorts of excellent viands ... and then you shall live freely there, without sergeants, or courtiers, or lawyers, or intelligencers, only a few industrious Scots perhaps, who indeed are dispersed over the face of the earth.

It all sounded very promising – even with the Scots.

Then, on 5 November 1605, the Catholic Guy Fawkes was found with some 36 barrels of gunpowder in a cellar under the Houses of Parliament, which put everything on hold for a while. Robert Cecil hunted down the plotters and usual suspects, and was rewarded with the title of Lord Salisbury, and in April 1606 a grateful King approved his proposal for two companies to colonise Virginia.

What of Captain John Smith all this while? There is nothing definite known of his activities after his return to England in 1604. Presumably he went back to Lincolnshire for a while; almost certainly he went to

London, where there were useful contacts to be made. Later, an enemy accused him of, at some unknown time, begging 'like a rogue without a licence' in Ireland. Whilst he would have had no need actually to beg, he could have gone to look for soldiering employment there, as many others did, or even with an eye to becoming a 'planter' there; but there is no evidence at all. He was certainly looking for something interesting to do: he writes that he had considered taking part in one of the expeditions to Guiana, following in Ralegh's wake, in either March 1604 or April 1605. Instead, he got involved with Bartholomew Gosnold.

Gosnold, former law student and privateer, from a 'good' Suffolk family, was related to Robert Bertie, Lord Willoughby, patron, like Peregrine Bertie, of John Smith. A friend of Ralegh, he was also linked by marriage to Thomas Smith, now grandly elevated to Sir Thomas Smythe, of the Muscovy, Levant and East India Companies, now returned from a stint as ambassador to Russia and looking for further investments. In the summer of 1605, Gosnold and Smith, the entrepreneur and the energetic, experienced soldier, met and began their collaboration.

As Smith wrote later, 'Captain Bartholomew Gosnold, the first mover of this plantation, having many years solicited many of his friends but found small assistance, at last prevailed with some gentlemen, as Master Edward-Maria Wingfield [another of Gosnold's kinsmen], Captain John Smith and divers others, who depended a year upon his projects; but nothing could be effected, till by their great charge and industry it came to be apprehended by certain of the nobility, gentry and merchants, so that His Majesty, by his letters patent, gave commission for establishing councils, to direct here [in England] and to govern and to execute there [Virginia].'

Gosnold, with Salisbury, Popham and Smythe behind him, did the diplomacy and negotiation; Smith, apart from his modest personal investment (£9), spent time and much of his money organising and recruiting suitable men (it was for others to recruit 'gentlemen'). He would have had some discussions with Hakluyt, a friend of Gosnold; he might have met Thomas Harriot and benefited from his work on the

Algonquian language, in which he early developed a facility. He probably met the navigator Henry Hudson (later to discover his own, epony-
mous Bay and River): Smith learned chart-making from someone, as his
maps – copies of which he sent to Hudson – demonstrate, and Hudson
seems a very likely teacher.

The stated objectives of the venture were to colonise and to establish
Christianity (Protestant, of course), to find a route through to 'the other
sea' and so to the Spice Islands, and – the Spanish had done it in South
America, so why not in the north? – to find gold. The Letters Patent
directed the colonists to 'dig, mine and search for all manner of mines
of gold, silver and copper'; one fifth of the gold and silver, and one fifteenth of the copper was to be reserved for the Crown. Some people,
such as Robert Gray in *A Good Speed to Virginia* (1609) asked, 'by what
right we can enter into the lands of these savages, take away their right-
ful inheritance from them, and plant ourselves in their place'. Hakluyt's
answer was that, as the English monarchs were Defenders of the Faith, it
was their duty 'also to enlarge and advance the same', bringing the people
to Christianity and civilisation. The Roman law principle of *res nullius*
was also deployed: land not fully used or occupied by one people could
rightfully be used by another people. The nomadic Indians 'ranged rather
than inhabited', Gray wrote cunningly, and so did not actually own any
particular part of the land: 'there is no *meum* and *tuum* [mine and thine]
amongst them, so that if the whole lands should be taken from them,
there is not a man that can complain of any particular wrong done him.'

As to the organization, there was a London-based council, with over-
sight of two companies, each with different bases and areas of opera-
tions. One, including Sir John Popham, Sir Humphrey Gilbert and Sir
Ferdinando Gorges (the Plymouth and Bristol nexus) was granted 'the
northern part of Virginia' – roughly, from modern Baltimore to Newfoundland – and concerns us no more. The other group, deriving from
London merchants and including Lord Salisbury, Sir Thomas Smythe,
the Revd Richard Hakluyt and Edward Maria Wingfield, another
kinsman of the Willoughbys and Veres and an experienced soldier who

intended to go to Virginia himself, got rights to 'southern Virginia' – again very roughly, from North Carolina to New York.

The initial commander until the colony was established was to be the 46-year-old Captain Christopher Newport, very experienced in Virginia voyages (he had been on John White's rescue mission of 1590) and privateering in the West Indies, where he had lost part of his right arm in a sea fight off Cuba attacking two Spanish treasure ships (he had also presented King James with two alligators from Santo Domingo). He would be master of the flagship, the *Susan Constant*, of 120 tons and a mere 76 feet long at the waterline. The second ship, the *God Speed*, 40 tons and 48 feet in length, was to be commanded by Bartholomew Gosnold; the third, a tiny 20-ton pinnace only 38 feet long, the *Discovery*, was commanded by one John Ratcliffe, of nothing is known except that he later claimed that he was also named Sicklemore. One is constantly amazed at the small size of the cockleshell craft that were launched to cross the great, stormy Atlantic – and how crowded they were: 71 people in the *Susan Constant*, 52 in the *God Speed* and 20 in the *Discovery*, to say nothing of animals, food supplies, water, tools and other equipment, arms, trade goods and personal possessions (more of these for the gentlemen). No room to swing a cat, indeed – but, unfortunately, room for anger and quarrels. Smith's *Generall Historie of Virginia* lists a total of 100 would-be settlers, or 'planters' as they were called, including 48 described as 'gentlemen', fussy about status and in general of little practical use. Another Thomas Smith wrote, in *De Republica Anglorum* (1583) 'whosoever studieth the laws of the realm, who studieth in the universities, who professeth liberal sciences, and, to be short, who can live idly and without manual labour ... he shall ... be taken for a gentleman'. Henry Peacham, in *The Compleat Gentleman* (1634), gives some idea what this meant: 'Noblemen and gentlemen ought to be preferred ... before the common people... . We ought to give credit to a nobleman or gentleman before any of the inferior sort... . They ought to take their recreations of hunting, hawking, etc freely, without control ... They may eat the best and daintiest meat that the place affordeth ...' The Revd Robert Hunt, 'a man not anyway to be touched with the rebellious humours of a popish spirit' (i.e., of somewhat Puritanical sympathies), chosen by Wingfield on the advice of the Archbishop of Canterbury, would tend their souls, Thomas Wotton and Thomas Wilkinson, surgeon, their bodies. The rest included carpenters, labourers, a blacksmith, a tailor and a drummer. There was to be a governing council of seven, but the names, in three sealed packets, one in each vessel, were not to be revealed until their arrival in Virginia. Until then, Newport was in charge.

Men had been recruited, food and supplies, trading goods, tools, armour and weapons had all been gathered (Hakluyt had prepared a list of everything needed for Roanoke, in 1585). There was an unfortunate beginning, perhaps ominous: the *Susan Constant*, moored in harbour at Ratcliffe in the Thames estuary, collided with another ship, causing considerable damage while, it was reported, the sailors 'sat tippling and drinking and never looked out or endeavoured to clear the ships'; more money was wasted in having to pay damages. Nevertheless, everything was ready. It was time to go.

In *Eastward Ho*, Captain Petronel Flash cries,

> Can we not reach Blackwall [downriver, now in Poplar, East London], where my ship lies, against the tide and in spite of tempests? Captains and gentlemen, we'll begin a new ceremony at the beginning of our voyage, which I believe will be followed of all future adventurers ... we'll have our provided supper brought aboard Sir Francis Drake's ship [at Deptford], that hath compassed the world: where with full cups and banquets we will do sacrifice for a prosperous voyage. My mind gives me that some good spirits of the water should haunt the desert ribs of her, and be auspicious to all that honour her memory, and will with like orgies enter their voyages.

So, on a chilly winter day, Smith and the others went downriver from the city, in wherries or tilt-boats, to Deptford, and then to Blackwall, and, on 29 December (new style; 19 December, old style), 1606, began their momentous voyage. The ships would have flown a new flag, that had been approved only that year, that combined the red cross of St George of England with the white-on-blue saltire cross of St Andrew of Scotland, to signify King James VI and I of Scotland and England. It seemed to everyone, in these sourer Jacobean times, like a renewal of the Elizabethan spirit of enterprise. The poet Michael Drayton cheered them on their way with a poem, 'To the Virginian Voyage':

> You brave heroic minds,
> Worthy your country's name,
> That honour still pursue,
> Go, and subdue,
> Whilst loitering hinds
> Lurk here at home with shame.

> Britons, you stay too long,
> Quickly aboard bestow you,
> And with a merry gale
> Swell your stretch'd sail
> With vows as strong
> As the winds that blow you.

> Your course securely steer,
> West and by south forth keep;
> Rocks, lee-shores, nor shoals,
> When Aeolus scowls,
> You need not fear,
> So absolute the deep.

> And cheerfully at sea,
> Success you still entice,
> To get the pearl and gold,

And ours to hold,
Virginia,
Earth's only paradise. ...

Thy voyages attend
Industrious Hakluit,
Whose reading shall inflame
Men to seek fame,
And much commend
To after times thy wit.

The voyage began badly. The 'good spirits of the water' were not
auspicious: as the little ships rounded the north-east corner of Kent
into the North Sea, great bitter winds blew against them, halting their
progress. For six whole weeks they remained, storm-tossed, riding at
anchor, only a few miles off-shore, in sight, ironically, of the Revd
Hunt's former home. Hunt was not a fortunate man: having joined
the expedition to further the word of God and his career, he feared
being cuckolded by his wife, Elizabeth. His will, made shortly before
he left, explicitly excluded her from inheriting if during his lifetime she
should 'commit the act of incontinency ... or ... stay and abide in one
and the same house ... with John Taylor'. Now, prostrate in the *Susan
Constant*, he suffered most terribly from seasickness, as well as criticism,
in the rancorous atmosphere generated by weeks of extreme discomfort,
frustration and smelly overcrowding among men of very different back-
grounds and outlooks.

Smith admired his fortitude: 'so weak and sick that few expected his
recovery. Yet ... notwithstanding the stormy weather, nor the scandalous
imputations of some few, little better than atheists, of the greatest rank
amongst us, suggested against him; all this could never force from him
so much as a seeming desire to leave the business, but he preferred the
service of God in so good a voyage before any affection to contest with
his godless foes, whose disastrous designs, could they have prevailed,

had even then overthrown the business, so many discontents did then arise.'

It is not clear what was behind all this. There may have been suggestions that Hunt, rather Puritanically inclined, was bad luck (Smith would have remembered his own experience off Nice); 'atheist' was mostly an abusive term, used loosely for anyone whose religious views differed from the speaker's. Smith probably had in mind Edward-Maria Wingfield, from a Catholic family, later President in Virginia, who later wrote that he was accused there of being 'an atheist, because I carried not a Bible with me, and because I did forbid the preacher to preach' (probably Puritanical sentiments). Another would have been Master George Percy, Wingfield's cousin and also of Catholic family, the youngest brother of Henry Percy, Earl of Northumberland (very grand family indeed – descendants of Harry Percy and Northumberland of Shakespeare's *Henry IV*). Percy kept a journal, to which we are indebted for accounts of the journey out and the early days of the colony. It is unlikely that they would have thought much of yeoman's son, John Smith.

At last the winds eased and they could get away, down the Channel and then southward towards the Canary Islands – not the direct route, but the most familiar (especially to Captain Newport) and easy, in order to cross the Atlantic driven by the easterly (what would later be called the 'trade') winds that had helped Columbus to the West Indies. *En route*, on 12 February, Percy records that they saw a 'blazing star', presumably Halley's Comet. By the time they reached the Canaries on about 17 February, relationships had deteriorated badly. In his *Generall Historie*, Smith relates how, from their departure from the Canaries, he 'was restrained as a prisoner, upon the scandalous suggestions of some of the chief (envying his repute), who feigned he intended to usurp the government, murder the council, and make himself king ... for this he was committed as a prisoner.' It sounds as though Wingfield had found Smith insufficiently deferential, even unbearably bumptious; exaggerated accusations and counter-accusations flew back and forth; and Newport bought some quiet by having Smith 'restrained' – though what form this took in such a cramped, crowded ship is not obvious.

Fair winds now took the little fleet westward: their next landfall was some 3,200 miles and 30 pleasantly tedious days away, at Martinique in the Windward Islands, and on 24 March they put in at Dominica for fresh water and supplies. Percy described it as 'very fair ... the trees full of sweet and good smells, inhabited by many savage Indians ... all painted red, to keep away the biting of mosquitoes'. In fact, the natives were not savage towards them: having overcome their fears (they had had bad experiences with the Spanish), they were happy to trade 'many kinds of fruits, as pines [pineapples], potatoes, plantains, tobacco' in exchange for copper, beads, knives and hatchets ('which they esteem much'). The fleet then sailed north, briefly visiting Guadeloupe, where they encountered a natural hot-water spring, 'so hot that no man was able to stand long by it. Our Admiral, Captain Newport, caused a piece of pork to be put in it; which boiled it so, in the space of half an hour, as no fire could mend it [have done better].'

Next, they called in at Nevis, in the Leeward Islands, on 28 March, intending a longer stay, to rest and recover. Percy describes it as 'all woody ... so thick ... you cannot get through it but by making your way with hatchets or falchions. Whether it was the dew of those trees, or of some others, I am not certain, but many of our men became so tormented with a burning swelling all over their bodies they seemed like scalded men, and near mad with pain. Here we found a great pool, wherein bathing themselves, they found much ease, and ... were well cured in two or three days.'

The men had hacked into manchineel trees, that have a burning, toxic sap and apple-like fruit; the Latin name, *Hippomane mancinella,* means, 'Little apple that drives horses mad'. Interestingly, Percy says nothing of what else flared up while they were there: Smith's enemies returned to the attack, renewing their accusations. Newport may have been away up-country, foraging, so giving Wingfield, as senior man there, the opportunity to try and condemn Smith. However, they were not now confined to the *Susan Constant,* and Smith would have had support from friends, such as Gosnold. As Smith recorded laconically, in his *True Travels,* 'A pair of gallows was made, but Captain Smith, for whom they were intended, could not be persuaded to use them.' For all that, he remained under restraint.

On they went, now westward past the Virgin Islands, to the little island of Mona, between Puerto Rico and Hispaniola (Newport knew this area very well, from his previous voyages). Here, on 7 April, the men changed the water, which had become foul and stinking, while a party of gentlemen went hunting: they killed some boar and 'a loathsome beast like a crocodile called a gwayn [iguana]', wrote Smith, but also endured their first fatality, from heat-stroke: 'Edward Brooke, gentleman, whose fat melted within him by the great heat and drought of the country,' as Percy wrote: 'We were not able to relieve him nor ourselves, so he died in that great extremity.' On nearby Moneta, after a difficult landing, they found the little island covered with birds (unfamiliar with men) and eggs, so that 'we were not able to set foot on the ground but either on fowls or eggs, which lay so thick in the grass'; they took 'near two hogsheads ... in three or four hours.'

Now it was time to head north, for Virginia, Drayton's 'earth's only paradise'. For ten days they sailed, past the Outer Banks, into an empty sea, with declining confidence; Ratcliffe of the *Discovery* and some others wanted to give up and sail home. 'But God,' wrote Smith, 'forcing them by an extreme storm to hull all night, did drive them by his providence to their desired port, beyond their expectations.' A few days later, in the dim light of four o'clock in the morning, a look-out sighted land. They had arrived in Chesapeake Bay (one can imagine Newport saying, 'I told you so.'). That morning, 26 April, their boats ran ashore on a sandy beach, still littered with the flotsam of the recent storms, bordered by a silent forest. There, wrote Percy, 'we could find nothing worth the speaking of, but fair meadows and goodly tall trees [Virginia in spring is heavily scented with dogwood, sumac and other blossoming trees], with such fresh waters running through the woods, as I was almost ravished at the first sight thereof.' Meanwhile, John Smith was still 'in restraint', a prisoner.

Getting to Know You

The first to land on what they called Cape Henry, after Henry, Prince of Wales, was a select party composed of Newport, Wingfield, Gosnold, Percy and Gabriel Archer, an ambitious friend of Gosnold, with a guard of soldiers. They spent the day exploring, finding 'nothing worth the speaking of'; they saw no Indians – but the Indians saw them. At dusk, as they prepared to board their boats, several Indians came, as Percy wrote, 'creeping upon all fours from the hills like bears, with bows in their mouths' (considering the size of the bows, quite a tricky feat), and suddenly shot at them. Archer and a sailor were wounded; the rest fired back, 'which the Indians little respected,' according to Smith, 'but having spent their arrows, retired without harm.' It was not the start that had been hoped for. As it happened, their choice of landing-spot was unfortunate: the natives there had unpleasant memories of being attacked by Spaniards in 1572, and were not inclined to discriminate between European tribes.

That night, it was time to open the box containing the list of names for the local governing council, with other instructions from the London company. The first of the seven names, unsurprisingly, was that of Captain Newport – but he would shortly be returning to England; then Gosnold, the initiator of the scheme, Wingfield, the senior soldier, Captain John Ratcliffe, who had subscribed £50 to the company, Captain

John Martin, son of Sir Richard Martin, goldsmith and thrice Lord Mayor of London, Captain George Kendall, there probably as a protégé of the Earl of Salisbury, and Captain John Smith, probably as a friend of Gosnold and protégé of Lord Willoughby. The last name would have come as an unpleasant shock to several there; but Smith was still under restraint, and for the time being still excluded.

Next came a reading of the London Council's generally sensible instructions: the party should take time in choosing a suitable site, which should not be too heavily wooded (to save labour in clearing), on a river (preferably one that would 'soonest find the other sea') with ready access for supply vessels but well upriver and away from the coast, and with a 'sconce' or outpost at the river-mouth, to prevent surprise attacks by the Spanish. The *Discovery* pinnace was to be retained for use in exploration. Having read reports of Spanish cruelty in South America, the Company made a point of advising the colonists to 'have great care not to offend the naturals', the local natives, whose friendly, or at least not actively hostile, assistance would be needed, both in obtaining food supplies and in exploring for gold and waterways through to the 'other sea'. They should be careful not to be deserted by any native guides, taking compasses with them on expeditions (this was to prove good advice), and, to keep the natives in awe, not let them see any poor marksmen in action, 'for if they see your learners miss what they aim at, they will think the weapon not so terrible, and thereby will be bold to assault you'. The Company had its investment very much in mind: once the site had been settled, Newport was to take 40 men upriver to look for gold and a route through to the other sea; and no-one was to send back to England any bad news or 'any letter of anything that may discourage others'.

The next morning, they put together a pre-fabricated small boat, a 'shallop' or barge of shallow draught, and a small group went some eight miles inland on the south side of the bay. They met no natives, but saw smoke, and came across a hastily-abandoned campsite, with oysters cooking, which they took: 'very large and delicate in taste', apparently. On 29 April, they set up a cross on the site of their first landing on Cape

Henry, and the day after went exploring again, and encountered five men in a canoe, 'at first very timorsome', who invited them to their village on the north bank, Kecoughtan, the home of the small Kecoughtan tribe. The men there were almost naked, with a small leather covering in front; some were painted red or black, their hair shaven on the right and grown three or four feet long on the left, tied with feathers, with sometimes a small, live, green and yellow snake as an ear-ring. Mats were spread on the ground, and an impromptu welcoming feast laid out; after this, the men performed a dance, stamping in time but with each dancer moving his body, hands and feet independently, 'shouting, howling and stamping against the ground ... making noise like so many wolves or devils'. Conversation at this stage was confined to signs and gestures – none of Newport's group seems to have benefited from Harriot's work. After the dance, Newport gave the Indians bells, beads and similar little gifts. The first semi-formal meeting of colonists and natives, a little party, seemed to have gone well.

Newport and his party spent a couple of weeks going up and down river (now called the James River), looking for a suitable place for the settlement, 'the most apt and securest place, as well for his company to sit down in as which might give the least cause of offence or distaste' to the natives, and visiting other villages and tribes. One werowance, or chieftain, welcomed them in full regalia of red deerskin hat, pearl necklace and bracelet, painted in blue and crimson and playing on a flute made of a reed; another tribe, however, met them with armed warriors and were not easily mollified. George Percy noticed one warrior carrying not only bow and arrows but 'pieces of iron to cleave a man in sunder'; the Indians could not smelt iron, so these must have had a European origin. He also saw 'a savage boy, about the age of ten years, which had a head of hair of a perfect yellow and a reasonable white skin, which is a miracle among savages' – he could well have been the descendant of a Roanoke colonist; but no inquiry was made.

On 12 May, they found a 'point of land', lightly wooded, with vines and turkeys, that Gabriel Archer thought was suitable, 'sufficient with a

little labour to defend ourselves against any enemy'. However, to Archer's chagrin, Wingfield rejected 'Archer's Hope' ('hope' meaning a small
space of land, or haven) and preferred a site a couple of miles upriver, a
low-lying peninsula, moderately wooded with cedar, maple, elm and ash,
about two miles by one mile in area, linked to the mainland by a narrow
sandbar ('a slender neck no broader than a man may well quoit a tile
shard', wrote William Strachey later, incidentally offering an unexpected
insight into early amusements), easily defensible, with the advantage of
a deep water frontage, where their ships could moor. Even Smith later
called it 'a very fit place for the erecting of a great city'. It seemed very
pleasantly situated; Percy described himself and a few others walking
in the woods, 'the ground all flowing over with fair flowers of sundry
colours and kinds, as though it had been in any garden or orchard in
England', with strawberry plants and sweet-scented trees 'like a paradise'.
Unfortunately, the site, which they decided to call 'Jamestown', had less
obvious drawbacks: considerable parts to the north and east were marshy
and even swampland (the Company had warned them, prophetically,
to avoid 'a low and moist place because it will prove unhealthful'); the
river here, even at nearly 60 miles from Cape Henry, was tidal, and the
river water, used for drinking, was brackish. Also, though the area was
deserted, it had been used as a hunting ground by the nearby Paspahegh
tribe, who would not be pleased.

On 14 May 1607 the colonists landed, and at last got round to swearing in six councillors, with 'an oration made, why Captain Smith was not
admitted of the council as the rest', as he noted; Wingfield was elected
President of the council, with two votes to the others' single votes. 'Now
falleth every man to work,' wrote Smith; some chopped down trees to
clear space – for tents only, at this stage – or cut wood into boards to be
exported to England; others prepared the ground for planting. Remembering the Company's instructions not to offend the natives, Wingfield
refused to build a fort of any kind, but George Kendall objected vigorously, and got a half-moon palisade of tree-branches set up, as a partial
defence. 'What toil we had with so small a power to guard our workmen

a-days, watch all night, resist our enemies, and effect our business, to reload the ships, cut down trees and prepare the ground to plant our corn, etc, I [Smith] refer to the reader's consideration.'

Within a few days messengers came, to announce that the Paspaheghs' werowance, Wowinchopunck, would be coming on a welcoming visit, with a present of a fat deer. Two days later he arrived with the deer, and 100 armed men – an intimidating sight, however they conducted themselves. He furthermore invited the colonists to lay aside their weapons, ostensibly as a sign of friendship, which they declined to do. He then went on, partly by signs, to raise the question of land usage, but before this could develop, one of his men picked up a hatchet lying nearby; a colonist snatched it back and hit the man on the arm; another Indian then 'came fiercely at our man with a wooden sword, thinking to beat out his brains'. Before it all got out of hand, Wowinchopunck led off his men 'in great anger'. Archer later claimed that the natives 'steal anything comes near them, yea, are so practised in this art that, looking in our face, they would with their foot, between their toes convey a chisel knife, piercer or any indifferent light thing, which having once conveyed, they hold it an injury to take the same from them.' Two days later, Wowinchopunck sent 40 men with another deer, apparently on a peace mission; they even asked to stay the night at the English camp, a request that was refused. Before they left, a gentleman set up a target, so thick that a pistol ball would not be able to penetrate it, and invited the Indians to have a go. Their bows, Percy reports, were made of 'tough hazel, their strings of leather, their arrows of canes or hazel, headed with very sharp stones'. To the astonishment of the English, the very first arrow, 'about an ell [45 inches] long' went right through, sticking out of the other side by about a foot; perhaps some of them began to get an idea of what they might be up against. To counteract this, they then set up a steel target, such as the Indians had not encountered; this time, the arrow broke into pieces. The Paspaheghs left in a bad temper.

Now Captain Newport got round to carrying out his last instructions from London; he was supposed to take Bartholomew Gosnold and 40 men upriver for two months, to search for gold or promising-looking waterways. In the event, he left Gosnold behind, and took only 18 sailors and five colonists, including Archer, Percy – and John Smith. Whatever others' complaints, Newport knew who would be a useful man to have in a dangerous situation. The weather was mild, the river broad and rippling over shallows; on land, there were flowering maples, Spanish chestnuts, cypresses, oaks, ash and vines, with soft fruits coming into season, and the calling of unfamiliar birds: it must have been rather pleasant. The shallop took them some 18 miles on the first day; the next day they hailed some Indians with 'wingapoh' (meaning 'friends') and asked them the way. After Archer showed them how to draw with pen and paper, one of them sketched a map of the waterway, indicating how far it was navigable (before some falls), two islands and then, farther off, some mountains. They pressed on, followed by the Indians, hopeful of a little more trading.

On 23 May, they were ceremoniously received by the werowance of the Arrohattocs, with venison and corn (village gardens were planted with gourds, pumpkins, peas, maize and tobacco); here they learned that the various tribes that they had met so far were in fact subordinate to a paramount chief (or mamanatowick) known as Powhatan, or Wahunsenacock. Born probably in the early 1540s, a forceful ruler, he had expanded the empire he had inherited from six to about twenty tribes, commanding over 3,000 warriors and some 8,000 people overall in most of modern eastern Virginia, receiving substantial tributes of food, furs, copper and pearls. He had, though the English did not know this yet, previous experience of Europeans.

In about 1561, a Spanish reconnaissance trip had entered Chesapeake Bay, and taken away with them an Indian youth, son of a chieftain, who was baptised as Don Luis Velasco and trained by Jesuits in Mexico, Spain and Havana as a go-between and guide for further expeditions. In 1570 a small Jesuit party returned with him, settling among unfriendly Indians not far from Jamestown; Don Luis soon disappeared amongst his own people, and shortly afterwards the mission was wiped out. A relief vessel was sent out, and then a punitive force in 1572, that ended by hanging several Indians. In 1588 a Spanish vessel sailed as far as the Potomac River, and kidnapped two boys. The Spanish were not well liked. Powhatan would also have known about the Roanoke people, and what had happened to them. In 1603, Bartholomew Gilbert's ship was driven by storms into either Chesapeake or Delaware Bay and had five crew-members killed. Another ship had arrived in 1605 or 1606; the captain killed a chief and kidnapped some men.

Shortly before the colonists arrived, one of Powhatan's priests had a prophetic vision, which indicated that a people would arise from the east, in Chesapeake Bay, that would cause the overthrow and destruction of his empire. The only people there at the time was the Chesapeake tribe: they were immediately exterminated. A second prophecy insisted that 'twice they should give overthrow and dishearten the attempts, and such strangers as should invade their territories or labour to settle a plantation amongst them, but the third time they themselves should fall into their subjection and under their conquest.' Powhatan knew about these new arrivals – one of his sons was ruler of Kecoughtan village; now he and his advisers would want to know if this little band composed the forerunners of the prophesied destroyers (unlikely as it seemed at the time, they were, of course).

While Newport and the others were relaxing after their meal, trying out the Arrohattocs' tobacco, the arrival of a great leader was announced; they thought it was Powhatan himself, though it was only his son, Parahunt, also known, confusingly, as Tanx Powhatan. The villagers rose respectfully to greet him, but the English ostentatiously remained seated, to demonstrate equality of status; Newport did, however, give the chief many presents, 'as penny knives, shears, bells, glass toys, etc', and departed on amicable terms. The group then went upriver as far as they could, with guides appointed by Parahunt; as they went they looked for signs of minerals, and Smith noted rocks 'of a gravelly nature, interlaced with many veins of glistering spangles'. At one island they were feasted by Parahunt, who told them that the tribes downriver by the entrance to the bay were unfriendly, which Archer confirmed, showing his arrow-wound. Parahunt then proposed a league of friendship (these new people might yet come in handy in a campaign against the opposition), and warned them against going any farther, as the Monacan tribe there was hostile. Newport thought that the 'other sea' might be only a few days' travel away, but acceded to Parahunt's wishes whilst contemplating a return trip with a larger force. At the base of the falls he set up a cross to claim the territory for King James; Parahunt was not sure what this action signified (they lied to him), but was not pleased. On 25 May the Arrohattoc werowance suffered his first hangover from English alcohol. Later, he asked to hear a musket fired, at which he 'stopped his ears and expressed much fear ... some of his people being in our boat leapt overboard at the wonder thereof'.

They then went downriver with an Arrohattoc guide named Nauirans, who later 'proved a very trusty friend'; they made their way slowly, stopping off for visits and feasting. They met the werowance of the Pamunkeys, Opechancanough (Powhatan's half-brother and possible heir), who invited Newport to stay the night; when he noticed Smith and others following them into the woods, he decided to return. They also met a woman werowance, described by Archer as 'a fat, lusty, manly woman', with even more 'majesty' than the male chiefs, and ostentatiously unimpressed by the sound of a musket; Smith was to meet her again later. Then, on 27 May, Nauirans suddenly declared that he had to go home; his abrupt departure, with that of one or two others, aroused their suspicions, and they hurried back to Jamestown – to a nasty surprise.

For a few days, the colonists in Jamestown had noticed frequent visits by Indians, in ones and twos, wandering about and inspecting the layout. Then, on the 26 May, they attacked in force, 200 or more: 'They came up almost into the fort,' (such as it was), wrote Archer, 'shot through the tents ... hurt 11 men (whereof one died after) and killed a boy.' The colonists were not properly armed (in accordance with Wingfield's policy, most of the weapons were stored away), but fought back as best they could; an arrow passed through Wingfield's beard, which must have been quite bushy, but did no harm. Then the ships moored alongside fired their cannon. 'Had it not chanced a cross-bar shot from the ships struck down a bough from a tree among them, that caused them to retire,' Smith wrote, 'our men had all been slain.'

After that, it was obvious that a proper fort would have to be built, immediately. When completed, it was of a good size, of triangular plan with wooden palisades (produced by clearing a lot more trees) with firing steps set on the inside, 140 yards long on the south or river side, with a central gate, and 100 yards long on each of the others; there were three bulwarks for their cannon, demi-culverins – medium size, about 4½ inches bore – and smaller sakers and falcons. In the middle were a store-house and guardroom, with tents or simple cabins. At first, as Smith recalled in *Advertisements*, their church (with common prayer twice a day, two sermons every Sunday – Revd Hunt earning his corn) was an old sail draped over three or four trees, with logs as seats; in bad weather they used an old, rotten tent. Later, they built 'a homely thing like a barn ... covered with sedge and earth'. On the central flagpole fluttered the new flag, of St George and St Andrew. By 15 June, the fort was finished, and most of their corn and seeds were sown.

While this went on, the surrounding Indians had continued sniping. On 31 May 'they came lurking in the thickets and long grass', firing arrows. Poor old Charles Clovill was shot with six arrows, dying eight days later; he was buried secretly within the fort, as was another man shot while 'going out to do natural necessity', so that the attackers should not know. There was increasing criticism of Wingfield's leadership, probably led by Smith, countered by arguments that Smith should be sent away, back to England. Newport and Hunt argued vigorously for reconciliation and harmony, and on 10 June Smith was sworn in as member of the council. A few days later, two friendly Indians arrived, and told them which tribes were likely to be friendly – the Arrohattoc, Pamunkey, Mattaponi and Youghtamund – and, unfortunately closer at hand, the unfriendly: the Paspahegh, Weyanock, Appomatoc, Kiskiack and Quiyoughcohannock. On their way out, they remarked that the colonists would be safer if they cut down the surrounding long grass and scrub, ideal bushes for ambushes; remarkably, this had not occurred to Wingfield and the other leaders. The grass was cut, and the attacks stopped.

Now it was time for Newport to go home, leaving Wingfield in charge. When Newport asked him how settled or confident he felt, Wingfield replied that 'no disturbance could endanger him or the colony but it must be wrought either by Captain Gosnold or Master Archer; for the one [Gosnold] was strong with friends and followers, and could if he would; and the other was troubled with an ambitious spirit, and would if he could.' Astonishingly, Newport then reported this to both men, urging them to 'be mindful of their duties to his Majesty and the colony'. The council now prepared a report for the London Council (carefully selective, like most committee reports), saying that 'within less than seven weeks, we are fortified well against the Indians, we have sown good store of wheat, we have sent you a taste of clapboard [they also sent two tons of sassafras for the suffering amorists of London], we have built some houses, we have spared some hands to a discovery [exploration]' – though not as many nor for as long as they were directed. They said they hoped for more support and supplies, encouraging hopes for gold and further success: 'We entreat your succours with all expedition, lest that all-devouring Spaniard lay his ravenous hands upon these gold-showing mountains.'

On Sunday 21 June they all took Holy Communion; the next day Newport and his sailors sailed off with the council's report and several other letters and reports (he promised to be back in 20 weeks), leaving behind about 100 colonists, 'very bare and scanty of victuals,' wrote Percy, 'furthermore in wars and in danger of the savages', left to their own resources to cope with a new life – and the surrounding watchful natives.

Tuftataffety Humourists

Within a few days of Newport's departure came messengers from the Pamunkeys' werowance, with a gift of a deer and offering friendship – and a polite inquiry as to where the ships (and their cannon) had gone; it seemed a good idea to tell them that they had gone to Croatoan. Then Powhatan sent a messenger also offering friendship and alliance – and what about those ships?

Now, with high summer coming on, the situation should have been very promising. The James River and Chesapeake Bay were well stocked with sturgeon and other fish – rockfish, perch, mullet, shad, eels, oysters and mussels; the land was fertile, with corn, nuts and berries growing, and plenty of game, from deer to turkey and squirrels. It was high time to be getting on with developing the settlement; but, it seems, nothing happened. An extraordinary passivity, or lethargy, set in. Whether made inert by debilitating illness, or by a sense of disorientating isolation and impotence in such alien circumstances, they did not build, nor hunt, nor dig; the gentlemen felt themselves above such labour; most people apparently just sat about and grumbled.

While the ships had been there, wrote Smith, 'our allowance was somewhat bettered by a daily portion of biscuit which the sailors would pilfer to sell, give or exchange with us for money, sassafras, furs or love. But when they departed, there remained neither tavern, beer-house nor place of relief but the common kettle [cooking-pot].' The daily ration was half a pint of boiled barley and half a pint of wheat, 'and this having fried some 26 weeks in the ship's hold, contained as many worms as grain' (first-class protein, mind you). With dry humour, he remarked, 'Had we been as free from all sins as [from] gluttony and drunkenness, we might have been canonised for saints,' but, he went on, 'our President would never have been admitted [to that state], for engrossing to his private [use] oatmeal, sack, oil, aqua vitae, beef, eggs or what not.' Wingfield would have had his own personal stores, that he would not expect to share, especially with the lower orders; the accusation of selfish hoarding, or worse, would return.

It was not long before hungry men on poor diet and bad water began to fall ill. 'It fortuned that within ten days scarce ten amongst us could either go, or well stand, such extreme weakness and sickness oppressed us.' Then the weakened men began to die.

'The sixth of August there died John Asbie of the bloody flux [dysentery]. The ninth day died George Flowre of the swelling. The tenth day died William Bruster, gentleman, of a wound given by the savages, and was buried the eleventh day. The fourteenth day, Jerome Alicock, ancient [ensign, junior officer], died of a wound, the same day Francis Midwinter, Edward Morris, corporal, died suddenly. The fifteenth day, there died Edward Browne and Stephen Galthorpe. The sixteenth day, there died Thomas Gower, gentleman. The seventeenth day, there died Thomas Mounslie. The eighteenth day, there died Robert Pennington, and John Martin, gentleman [son of councillor John Martin]. The nineteenth day, died Drue Pigasse, gentleman.'

George Percy provides a dreadful picture. 'Our men were destroyed with cruel diseases, as swellings, fluxes, burning fevers and by wars, and some departed suddenly, but for the most part they died of mere famine. There were never Englishmen left in a foreign country in such misery as we were in this newly discovered Virginia. We watched every three nights lying on the bare, cold ground, what weather soever ... our drink cold water taken out of the river, which was at a flood very salt, at a low tide full of slime and filth, which was the destruction of many of our men ... Some departing out of the world many times three or four in a night, in the morning their bodies trailed out of their cabins like dogs to be buried.'

John Smith and Ratcliffe both fell ill, but recovered. Remarkably, Wingfield alone did not fall ill; no wonder there was comment. Then Bartholomew Gosnold, founder, and kinsman of Wingfield, died on 22 August, with a formal burial ceremony. 'In his sickness time,' wrote Wingfield, 'the president did early foretell his own deposing from command, so much differed the president and the other councillors on managing the government of the colony.'

Things got worse; both Smith and Wingfield later wrote that there were not six able-bodied men in the fort: the Indians could have walked in. In late August, George Kendall was charged with 'heinous' conduct (unspecified: an ambitious troublemaker, he probably stirred up more dissension than could be endured), removed from the council, and confined to the pinnace; the council was down to four. Some temporary salvation appeared. Powhatan, not realising how weak the English were (all the dead had been buried secretly within the fort, the shallow graves probably contributing to the spread of infection), now used the early harvest (perhaps the food was there, had they gone and got it) to trade corn for beads and hatchets, so sparing them from collapse and death.

Wingfield extended rationing, whilst complaining that a chicken from his private stock was mysteriously 'spirited away'; later he wrote, implausibly, that he had bred more than 37 chickens but eaten only one, while Ratcliffe had eaten four or five. By the second week in September at least 42 colonists had died of disease or malnutrition. In later years, recalling the struggles at the beginning of the colony, Wingfield wrote, 'I bethought me of the hard beginnings which in former times betided those worthy spirits that planted the greatest monarchies in Asia and Europe; wherein I observed rather the troubles of Moses and Aaron, with other of like history, than that venom in the mutinous brood of Cadmus, or that harmony in the sweet consent of Amphion.'

In Exodus 16, Moses and Aaron had to endure the 'murmurings' of the children of Israel; but there were no quails or manna to relieve Wingfield's situation. When Cadmus of Thrace, in ancient Greece, went to found the city of Thebes, he slew a great dragon and planted its teeth, which sprouted up as armed men, who fought amongst themselves until only five were left, who then helped to build the city. Later, Amphion, King of Thebes, seeking to build a new city, caused the building-stones to rise and fit together in response to his magical music. Wingfield, however, could not conquer the dragon of disease, recruit his quarrelling men, or create harmony. The inadequacy of his leadership was all too apparent, and on 10 September, Martin, Ratcliffe and Smith presented him with a signed warrant dismissing him from the council and his presidency. Telling them loftily that 'they had eased him of a great deal of care and trouble' (see if I care), he concluded, 'I am at your pleasure, dispose of me as you will without further garboil [fuss]'; he was sent to join Kendall in restraint in the *Discovery*.

The next day, there was a general assembly, with Ratcliffe as the new president, and Archer as secretary, of whom Wingfield wrote that it was 'natural to this honest gent Master Archer to be always hatching of some mutiny; in my time, he might have appeared an author of three several mutinies'. Archer was to take aim at other leaders later. Only Wingfield gives any details of the proceedings, in his report to the London Council, in which he insists that the charges against him were petty or absurd. Ratcliffe, he wrote, complained that he had 'denied him a penny whistle, a chicken, a spoonful of beer, and served him with foul corn'. Martin was more serious, saying 'that I do slack the service in the colony, and do nothing but tend my pot, spit and oven, but he [Wingfield] hath starved my son [John, recently dead] and denied him a spoonful of beer', and threatened him that his London friends would take revenge on him if he ever dared go there. Wingfield insisted that he had distributed the food allowances properly, and not secretly hoarded supplies, protesting feebly and ineffectually, 'I never had but one squirrel roasted, whereof I gave part to Master Ratcliffe, then sick; yet was that squirrel given me', whilst his private stock was only 'two glasses with salad oil which I brought with me out of England'. Smith had more important accusations, that Wingfield had accused him of lying and of concealing intended mutiny on the journey out; these charges would come back again. Wingfield's class arrogance was unfortunately apparent, as well as his disastrously mangled grammar, in his report: 'I said, though we were equal here, yet if he were in England he would think scorn his man should be my companion': if 'he' were replaced by 'I' and perhaps 'his' by 'this', his intended insult would be clearer. Ratcliffe then asked, unwisely, whether Wingfield would accept their authority, or appeal to the King; Wingfield naturally said he would appeal, and was sent back to the *Discovery*, whilst Kendall was released.

Smith described his fellow councillors as 'little beloved, of weak judgement in dangers, and less industry in peace'; however that may have been, Smith, as a practical man, was given 'the managing of all things abroad', and set himself to preparing the settlement for the coming winter, 'who, by his own example, good words and fair promises, set some to mow, others to bind thatch, some to build houses, others to thatch them, himself always bearing the greatest task for his own share, so that in short time he provided most of them lodgings, neglecting any for himself.' Credit where it is due, Smith obviously felt.

On 17 September, Wingfield was on trial again: a gentleman named Jehu Robinson claimed that Wingfield had been saying that Robinson and others had agreed with him to sail off in the pinnace to Newfoundland. Smith's accusations, of Wingfield giving him the lie and of a slander of concealing intended mutiny, came up again. Ratcliffe appointed a jury, who predictably found Wingfield guilty, and awarded £100 damages to Robinson and £200 to Smith, which he donated to the settlement. Wingfield also had to give up his personal kettle.

Having apparently got matters settled in Jamestown, Smith now had to organise more food. As 'Cape Merchant' or trade and supply officer, the best he had to trade with was, he wrote, little iron chisels, though still many there 'would rather starve and rot with idleness than be persuaded to do anything for their own relief without restraint'. Upriver he then went in the barge, with a small party, only to find the natives, realising the colonists' need, now offering very poor rates of exchange. His accounts indicate different methods applied at different times.

On one occasion, a gentle tactic worked well, when, confronted with unsatisfactory offers, he simply gave little presents to the village children, before returning to the barge overnight. In the morning, he sent a man ashore to fetch fresh water, when the villagers invited him ashore and traded fish, oysters, bread, venison and corn for his iron, beads and copper. On his way back, two men in canoes sought him out and traded fourteen bushels of corn.

On another occasion, when he was treated scornfully with derisive offers, he 'let fly his muskets, and ran his boat on shore, whereat they all fled into the woods. So marching towards their houses, they [his men] might see great heaps of corn. Much ado he had to restrain his hungry soldiers from present taking of it, expecting, as it happened, that the savages would assault them, as not long after they did, with a most hideous noise. Sixty or seventy of them, some black, some red, some white, some parti-coloured, came in a square order singing and dancing out of the woods, with their Okee (which was an idol made of skins, stuffed with moss, all painted and hung with chains and copper) borne before them; and in this manner, being well armed with clubs, targets [shields], bows and arrows, they charged the English, that so kindly received them with their muskets loaded with pistol shot, that down fell their god, and divers lay sprawling on the ground.' The rest fled into the woods, before sending an envoy to plead for peace and their Okee. So Smith was able to trade the Okee, beads, copper and hatchets at an acceptable rate for venison, turkeys, wildfowl and bread; the natives did a farrewell dance, and all parted reasonably satisfied. Smith was building a reputation among the natives.

It was then agreed that he should go upriver again, with the pinnace and the barge, to Powhatan's village, to trade for corn. On the way he called in at the Paspaheghs, never very friendly ('that churlish and treacherous nation'), who traded ten or twelve bushels, but also tried to steal some guns and swords, which caused an unpleasant scene, before, suspecting that they might attack, he returned to base. He then went farther, in quest of the Chickahominy River, that might lead to promising waterways, and the Chickahominy tribe that, being relatively distant and semi-independent of Powhatan, might be friendly – which they were. Smith bought from several villages, but each time only in small quantities, 'lest they should perceive my too great want' (good sense, both commercially and politically). When the barge was loaded, he went back for the agreed rendezvous with the pinnace, but could not find it; returning to Jamestown, he was told that the pinnace had got stuck in the mud. The next day, he took the barge up to the Chickahominies again, who were waiting with over 300 baskets. He seems to have got on well with them, particularly in improving his knowledge of the language (he seemed to have the soldier's knack of picking up useful phrases).

When he got back to base, it turned out that the pinnace's unavailability had not been entirely accidental. Smith's and Wingfield's versions of what happened do not altogether agree, as one might expect. It appears that, while Smith was away, President Ratcliffe had beaten James Read, the colony's blacksmith, who struck back (Smith says that he only 'offered to strike'): as Ratcliffe was now technically the King's representative, this was a capital crime. Only when Read actually faced the gallows did he save himself, by declaring that Kendall had tried to get a group (perhaps including his former fellow prisoner, Wingfield) to give up this increasingly chilly, hand-to-mouth existence, quietly load the pinnace and sail off in it. The *Discovery* had been all ready to go, which was why it had been kept from Smith. In his version, he 'unexpectedly returning had the plot discovered to him; much trouble he had to prevent it, till with store of saker [light cannon] and musket shot he forced them to stay or sink in the river.'

However that may be, at the trial Kendall admitted his scheme, even that he had intended to sell the location of the settlement to the Spanish. Condemned to death, he was granted the gentleman's privilege of death by firing-squad rather than on the gallows. Smith later wrote that 'the President and Captain Archer not long after intended also to have abandoned the country, which project also was curbed and suppressed by Smith.' When this happened, is not clear. Wingfield did write that, after Kendall's death, he had proposed going back to London himself, to 'acquaint our Council there with our weakness' (particularly, one suspects, with his treatment by Smith and his other critics), but not with Ratcliffe and Archer, and that he had been prepared to contribute £100 to the cost of taking back the whole colony – which sounds very like a bribe – an offer that was emphatically refused.

Smith had got in a reasonable stock of food, mostly from the Chickahominies. Now, in late autumn, the skies and waters were filled with water fowl: oystercatchers, mallard, teal, widgeon, shelduck, cranes, swans and geese. In the area round about were plover, snipe, woodcock and turkeys, as well as deer, beaver and bear. As he wrote, 'the winter approaching, the rivers became so covered with swans, geese, ducks and cranes that we daily feasted with good bread, Virginia peas, pompions [pumpkins] and putchamins [persimmons], fish, fowl and divers sorts of wild beasts, as fast as we could eat them: so that none of our tuftataffety humourists [pretentious whingers] desired to go for England' – or, if they did, they had the good sense to keep quiet about it, for a while.

For all this natural plenty, there was still discontent (and perhaps a desire to have Captain Smith out of the way), surfacing as complaints that he had not gone far enough in his explorations past the Chickahominies, to where there might be gold, or good waterways through to the other sea; and so, early that December, he set off again, with only nine men, on an expedition that, in his much later accounts, would make him, though in ways that he would not have expected or relished, famous.

Time of Trial

Early in an icy-cold December, Smith, accompanied by only Jehu Robinson (no friend of Wingfield, but perhaps therefore of Smith), Thomas Emry, a carpenter, George Cassen, a labourer, and six others, took the barge 40 miles upriver, into an area with many oozy marshes, rich in bird life, well populated, with fertile fields: 'a better seat for a town cannot be desired'. The river then began to be choked with little low islands; after Apokant, 'the highest town inhabited', it was blocked by a fallen tree, which they had to hack through, and became increasingly narrow and shallow. It was clear that he could not risk the boat any farther, so he returned to Apokant, to hire a canoe and guides, under the pretence of going fowling. The next day, he, Robinson and Emry went back up with two guides, leaving the others with strict orders not to go ashore.

His suspicions as to the friendliness of the natives, and the common sense of the others, proved well founded. Shortly after his departure, some men went ashore, perhaps attracted by Indian women, and one, George Cassen, was taken by surprise and captured. The Indians, not believing Smith's story of a wild-goose chase, interrogated him as to what Smith was up to. How long he resisted, we do not know, but, as they themselves later reported, they tied him to a tree and, as was common practice with captured enemies, with sharpened mussel shells sawed through the joints of his fingers and toes one by one, throwing the bits into the fire. Then, with the shells and sharp-edged reeds they slowly peeled off the skin from his head and face, before working down his body and ripping open his belly for his guts to fall out. Finally, heaping up some brushwood, they set fire to him. Some of them attacked the barge, but the remaining six Englishmen got away downriver, to report the deaths of Cassen, Smith and the rest; others, the smell of burning wood and flesh still in their nostrils, set off upriver, after Smith and his companions.

In the meantime, Smith and the others had got 20 miles up river, paddling with difficulty through shallow streams and marshes. At last finding some solid ground, he decided to go ashore; telling Emry, Robinson and one Indian to stay and start a cooking fire, he and the other Indian went off through the forest to inspect the land and look for the previously mentioned wildfowl. Robinson and Emry were told to have their muskets to hand, with matches at the ready; at any sign of danger they were to fire, as a signal for him to return.

After barely a quarter of an hour, he heard 'a loud cry and hallooing of Indians', but no gunshot. A large force of Indians, led by Opechancanough, the chief of the Pamunkeys, searching through the windings of the river, had surprised Robinson and Emry in a silent attack; afterwards, Smith was shown Robinson's body with 20 or 30 arrows in it. There was no sign of Emry or the other Indian.

Realising that he was under attack, and suspecting that his guide – who urged him to run for it – had betrayed him, Smith tied the Indian to his side by his garters, to use him as a shield. He was beset by a large number of warriors; an arrow struck him on his right thigh, causing only minor injury through his thick winter clothing. He fired his pistol – of a superior French make – but missed. While reloading, more arrows struck him. He fired again, with some success, and the attackers retreated, before a great host reinforced them, surrounding him and his guide threateningly. The guide called out that Smith was a werowance (chiefs were not to be killed, but kept as hostages; this also improved the guide's chances). His attackers demanded his surrender, offering his life for his gun. As he continued to back towards the canoe, his eyes on his enemies, he stepped into an icy 'quagmire' and fell in up to his middle, dragging his poor guide with him; unable to get out, he threw away his gun, and surrendered. The Indians hauled them out and took them to the fire in the clearing where Robinson's body lay, and set about rubbing and chafing his chilled legs, before dragging him off to Opechancanough. Smith had met him before, on Newport's trip up river, where he had impressed people by his stately manner; about 60 years old, he was second in line of succession to Powhatan.

Somehow Smith had to persuade this man that he was indeed of chieftain status, and to be spared. Remembering that the natives were very impressed by European technology, he produced his round ivory compass that, as the Council had advised, he had kept with him. As he slowly turned it, he showed them how the needle and card remained mysteriously, 'magically' pointing in the same direction, and, while clearly visible, yet could not be touched, because of the transparent glass. With this, he began an extraordinary lecture, discoursing, he later wrote, on 'the roundness of the earth, and skies, the sphere of the sun, moon and stars [pre-Copernican astronomy], and how the sun did chase the night round the world continually, the greatness of the land and sea, the diversity of nations, variety of complexions, and how we were to them antipodes, and many other like matters.'

How much of this rigmarole he was able to communicate, with his relatively limited knowledge of Algonquian, is doubtful; he says that they 'all stood as amazed with admiration'. For all that, within an hour they had tied him to a tree and gathered round him, ready to shoot him, as he presumed (at that time he did not know about the fun they had with mussel shells).

However, Opechancanough had been thinking. Perhaps he had been impressed by Smith's steady nerve; perhaps Smith was a werowance and not to be killed summarily. It might be useful to learn more from him, by one means or another, about the English strengths and weaknesses, and, especially, what their long-term intentions were. Perhaps Powhatan should see him. Taking the ivory compass – 'that globe-like jewel' – he held it over Smith's head, as a sign; the bows and arrows were lowered; execution was deferred.

Off they marched, to a nearby temporary hunting village, an advance guard carrying their captured guns and swords going before, then Smith, held by the arms, with six men in file on each side, 'their arrows nocked'. At the village, with 'all the women and children staring to behold him', the warriors did a counter-marching display, in single file, before encircling Smith and Opechancanough in a dance, 'singing and yelling out such hellish notes and screeches, being strangely painted, every one his quiver of arrows, and at his back a club; on his arm a fox or otter's skin or some such matter for his vanbrace [armguard]; their heads and shoulders painted red with oil and pocones [a vegetable dye] mingled together, which scarlet-like colour made an exceedingly handsome show; his bow in his hand, and the skin of a bird with her wings abroad dried, tied on his head, a piece of copper, a white shell, a long feather, with a small rattle growing at the tails of their snakes tied to it, or some such like toy.'

After three rounds of this, Smith was taken to a long house, guarded by 30 or 40 'tall fellows', and 'more bread and venison was brought him than would have served twenty men'. Perhaps not surprisingly, 'his stomach at that time was not very good'. At midnight they offered him the food again, and again the next morning, 'which made him think they would fat him to eat him' (there were in fact no cannibals in the area). Instead, an Indian to whom he had previously given some toys and beads when they first arrived in Jamestown brought him his cloak, to comfort him in the bitter cold; by contrast, the father of a young brave whom Smith had wounded in the skirmish tried to kill him, but was prevented. Though he could tell that the young man was dying, Smith said that he had some medicine in Jamestown that might cure him, if they would let him fetch it, but they were not so naïve as to permit that.

Opechancanough came and talked to him, asking about the English ships, obviously to learn what the Indians were up against; in exchange, he told Smith of the extent of Powhatan's empire, and how at a place called Ocanahonan there were men dressed like the English (perhaps the remains of the doomed Roanoke colony – if they existed at all), whilst in another direction, four or five days' journey away, there was a 'great turning of salt water', which Smith would have hoped was the longed-for Pacific – but was probably only salt springs. Meanwhile, plans went ahead for an attack on Jamestown, Opechancanough offering 'life, liberty, land and women' in return for his help.

As they were getting on so well, Smith suggested that he should send a message to the fort, to tell them how well he had been treated, 'lest they should revenge my death' (he was always keen to suggest the colonists' military power). Opechancanough agreed – it was at least a chance for his men to assess the situation at the fort. The message, on a page from Smith's notebook, in fact told the others of the intended attack, that they should intimidate the messengers with a show of strength (he had already alarmed them with stories of booby-traps, concealed mines and great guns), and also send him various necessaries, probably presents for his captors. In 'as bitter weather as could be of frost and snow', the three nervous messengers set off through the woods. When they got to Jamestown, seeing men sally out as he had told them they would, they ran off, leaving the letter, but on going back that night they got a better reply, including the things he had asked for. On their return, Smith read out (part of) the reply, to general amazement: either Smith could divine, or the paper could somehow speak.

Shortly after this, Opechancanough decided to move Smith around, perhaps to thwart any rescue party, parading him through various villages. In one, Powhatan's half-brother, the chieftain Kekataugh, feasted him, then apparently artlessly asked him to fire his admirable pistol at a target. Smith noticed that the target was set up a good 120 paces away, at roughly the upper limit of the natives' arrows, but beyond the range of his pistol. Concerned to conceal the limitations of the Englishmen's weapons, he covertly broke the cock of the pistol, and regretfully reported that it had got broken. At the next village, to the north, on the Rappahannock River, he was again exhibited to the people. Apparently, some years before, a ship – perhaps Spanish – had visited the area, when, despite having been treated well, the captain had killed the local chieftain; as it happened, the captain, whoever he was, had been a tall man, and Smith clearly was not. Soon – it was now nearly the end of December – he was brought to another village, for formal examination.

A great fire was made in the long house, with two mats set out, on one of which he was to sit. Immediately 'came skipping in a great grim fellow, all painted over with coal mingled with oil, and many snakes' and weasels' skins stuffed with moss, and all their tails tied together so as they met on the crown of his head in a tassel; and round about the tassel was as a coronet of feathers, the skins hanging round about his head, back and shoulders, and in a manner covered his face; with a hellish voice, and a rattle in his hand.'

The 'fellow', the chief priest, and his colleagues, then began an elaborate ritual, dancing and chanting, laying out kernels of corn in circles, with sticks and ground cornmeal in careful patterns. For three days this went on, with speeches and gestures, the chief 'straining his arms and hands with such violence that he sweat and his veins swelled'. The object, they explained, was to divine whether his intentions were benevolent, or not. The circle of meal signified their country, the circles of corn the limits of the sea, and the sticks his country. They imagined the world to be round and flat, with them in the middle. They also showed him a bag of gunpowder they had acquired, that they were keeping to plant in the spring.

At last Opechancanough brought him to Werocomoco village, the court of the supreme chief, Powhatan, on what is now the York River, little more than a dozen miles from Jamestown as the crow flies (the site was discovered in 2003). Here he was made to wait outside the long house, where 'more than two hundred of those grim courtiers stood wondering, as if he had been a monster', while Powhatan and his immediate suite prepared themselves; then he was led in.

As he entered, there was a sudden great shout from the assembled company. Then, through the wood smoke, he saw Powhatan, seated before the fire upon a pile of ten or twelve mats about a foot high; a tall, well-built man, with a severe expression, grey hair, scanty beard, between 60 and 80 years old ('a goodly old man ... though well beaten with many cold and stormy winters,' wrote William Strachey), hung with many pearl necklaces and covered with raccoon skins. On each side was a young woman of 16 or 18 (presumably his current concubines, who would stay with him until they bore him a child); along each side of the house sat two rows of men, with an equal number of women behind them, their heads and shoulders painted red, adorned with feathers and necklaces of white beads.

The queen (werowansquaw) of Appomatoc, 'a fat, lusty, manly woman' (as Archer described her), whom he had met before, brought him water to wash his hands, and another woman brought him a bunch of feathers, to dry them. Powhatan welcomed him with great platters of food, and began by assuring him of his friendship. He said how pleased he had been to hear Opechancanough's account of their conversation, before getting to the point: why had the English come to his kingdom? Obviously, the real reason, colonisation, had to be concealed. Smith told him that they had been in a battle with their enemies, the Spanish, been overpowered and forced to retreat, and driven by bad weather to land at Chesapeake Bay. The natives there had shot at them, but the people at Kecoughtan had treated them well; when the crew had asked by signs for fresh water, they were directed up river, where the people of Paspahegh (the site of Jamestown) had treated them 'kindly'. As their pinnace was leaky, they had to stay to mend her and wait for Smith's 'father', their leader, Admiral Newport, to come for them.

Why then, asked Powhatan, had they gone farther upriver, some months ago? Smith replied, that later he would have occasion to talk to him about the 'back' sea and how they might get there, but in the meantime (shifting to the attack) another 'child' of Admiral Newport – Robinson – had been killed, which they were determined to avenge. The implication was clear: killings of Englishmen were followed by puni-tive raids by more, vengeful, armed Englishmen (a familiar idea for the

Indians: Strachey wrote that 'they seldom make wars for land or goods, but for women and children, and principally for revenge').

On reflection, Powhatan replied that it was a different tribe responsible for the killing, and that he, not the English, would undertake any punishment. There were other savage tribes in the area, notably the Pocoughtaonack, cannibals with shaven heads with long hair behind, who fought with battle-axes and warred with other tribes. He went on to suggest the scope of his empire, and – presumably in answer to a question – to hint that he knew where Ralegh's men had landed, several days' journey to the south. In response, Smith discoursed on the breadth of Europe's nations, the power of King James and his navy, and the fierce fighting skills of Admiral Newport.

It was time for a decision: 'a long consultation was held'. Smith was clearly a strong character, not easily cowed: he could be a threat, the forerunner of a disastrous foe, or he could be an ally in dealing with recalcitrant tribes on the fringes of Powhatan's empire. He could be killed, befriended, or adopted into the tribe.

Two great stones were dragged in; as many as could get at Smith, seized him and dragged him to the stones, forced his head down and raised their clubs, poised to smash his skull. Then there was an interruption. Among the crowd was one of Powhatan's daughters (from one of his many wives), a girl of about ten or eleven, called Pocahontas – 'little wanton', not her proper name, which was Matoaka – known as her father's favourite. She cried out in protest at the execution, and then, 'when no entreaty could prevail', ran forward, 'got his head in her arms, and laid her own upon his to save him from death'. Powhatan gave the signal to halt.

No one is sure exactly what happened, or what it all meant. Was it as it seemed to Smith, a spontaneously interrupted execution? Was it, as has been suggested, a ritual of symbolic death of an old self and rebirth as a member of the tribe? Did it even happen at all?

The latter doubt was first expressed by the American writer Henry Adams in 1867, shortly after the Civil War. The Northerners, of whom

Adams was one, wanted to depreciate the status of the Southern states, and especially of Virginia, that could claim to be the foundation place of the United States, and to promote instead that of Massachusetts and the Pilgrim Fathers. The accusation that Smith invented the incident derives from his delay in mentioning it. His letter from Virginia, brought back by Captain Nelson and edited by someone else for publication as *A True Relation* in 1608, makes no mention of his rescue by the little girl (though Smith would have wanted to downplay the incident, both in accordance with the Company's direction that bad reports should not be made, and because it reflected no great credit on such a macho adventurer). In his own *Map of Virginia* in 1612, there is still no mention of the incident, though he does refer to her by name, confirming that she was 11 or 12 years old at most when they met, and denying absurd and ill-informed suggestions that he had hoped to have made himself king by marrying Powhatan's daughter (the laws of succession were, that no son inherited, but the brothers in turn, then the sisters, then the sisters' heirs); he does refer to the time when she came at night to warn him of an intended ambush. It is not until his *Generall Historie of Virginia* of 1624 that the story appears in print, when he refers to a letter he wrote to Queen Anne when Pocahontas visited England in 1616.

Sceptics have also pointed to a story, included by Hakluyt in 1609, which Smith could have read, of a Spaniard, Juan Ortiz, captured by Indians in Florida in 1528, condemned by the chief to be burned alive but spared at the request of the chief's delightfully-named daughter, Ulalah, and her mother and sister, and kept as a slave: Pocahontas, perhaps, could have been conflated with Trabigzanda, for a good story.

On the other hand, this comparable incident suggests that there might have been a convention of intervention, and that such a ritual of death and rebirth was not uncommon among the seaboard tribes. Certainly it seems improbable that with so many remarkable experiences in an action-packed life to narrate – and where it has been possible to check, his writings have seemed honest – Smith would cook up such a story, that would not reflect well on himself (one of his main concerns).

It seems likely that it was indeed a kind of ritual theatre, designed to gain a psychological hold on Smith, owing his life to Powhatan's generosity, and so make him a grateful member of the tribe and more inclined to act as a helpful intermediary.

In the meantime, something had to be done. It was suggested, probably by Pocahontas, that she could keep him, to make bells, beads and copper ornaments for her. This was not a serious suggestion. Proceedings were halted for a couple of days, presumably for further discussion.

William Strachey, in his *Historie of travell into Virginia Britannia* (1612), relates an incident reported to him by Smith, who appears not to have written about it himself, how Powhatan 'caused certain malefactors (at what time Capt Smith was prisoner with them, and to the sight whereof Capt Smith for some purpose was brought) to be bound head and foot' and burned to death in a pit of burning coals. Powhatan's 'purpose' would have been to intimidate with a demonstration of ruthless power, but whether before or after their 'strange and fatal interview' is not known.

After two days, guards brought Smith to a great house in the woods, and sat him there on a mat in front of a fire, all alone. Suddenly, from behind a mat hanging across the middle of the house, came 'the dolefullest noise he ever heard', and Powhatan appeared, painted black, and looking 'more like a devil than a man', accompanied by a throng equally fearsome in appearance. He told Smith that they were now friends, and that he could go back to Jamestown; he would give him the land of Capahowosick and 'esteem him as his son Nantaquoud' (in effect making him a werowance under him, and subject to him in the tribe). In return, Smith should give his new 'father' two cannon and a grindstone. Smith agreed.

Early on 1 January, he went off with a few guards commanded by Powhatan's trusted warrior, Rawhunt, to take the colonists some food and carry back the cannon and grindstone. Although Jamestown was only a few miles away through the woods, Rawhunt insisted on camping and feasting on the food supplies overnight (Smith still half expecting a last-minute killing). The next morning, they arrived at Jamestown, where he was greeted with delight. 'Each man,' he wrote, 'with the truest signs of joy they could express welcomed me' (some, it was to appear, less whole-heartedly than others). He 'used the savages with what kindness he could', and showed Rawhunt two demi-culverins (each weighing 3,000–4,000 lbs) and a millstone; carefully chosen, they were all too heavy for the Indians to carry. To impress them, he loaded the cannon with stones and fired them at a great tree, the branches of which were heavily laden with long icicles; with a mighty roar, the icicles and branches came crashing down, 'that the poor savages ran away half dead with fear'. Having coaxed them back, he gave them toys and presents for Powhatan, his women and children, 'as gave them in general full content'. Whether or not they were indeed content, and what they and Powhatan said to each other on their return, is not known; but that was what they had to settle for; and the cannon, the grindstone and Captain John Smith were all staying in Jamestown.

For Smith, however, the busy day was not yet over. Poor George Cassen's surviving comrades had got back to report the latest Indian attack and Smith's almost certain death. Gabriel Archer took the opportunity to get old John Martin to swear him in, against the constitution, as a replacement member of the council, a position conferring status and authority (and some payment). Now, in the midst of a bitter winter, with fewer than 40 of the original colonists left alive, it again seemed a good idea to get out and back to England. Smith reports how 'Now in Jamestown they were all in combustion, the strongest preparing once more to run away with the pinnace; which, with the hazard of his life, with saker, falcon and musket shot [and the support of the handful who would have been left behind, at the mercy of the natives] Smith forced now the third time to stay or sink'.

There was a prompt counter-attack, not by arms (Smith could be expected to defeat that) but with an extraordinary 'legal' charge: that Smith, in taking Robinson and Emry with him into danger, was responsible for their deaths (echoes of Michael Williams's criticism in

Shakespeare's *Henry V*). Consequently, by application of Levitical law (particularly Leviticus 24:17–21, 'eye for eye, tooth for tooth: As he hath caused a blemish in a man, so shall it be done to him again ... He that killeth a man, he shall be put to death'), Smith should be executed. The trial was held that very day: Ratcliffe and Archer had three votes between them; Smith was sentenced to be hanged the next day, 'so speedy,' as Wingfield wrote, 'is our law there'.

Then, late that evening, 2 January, there was a shout from the lookout: there, out of the gathering darkness, loomed a strange ship. Fortunately, it was not Spanish, but the *John and Francis*, after a stormy 12 weeks and two days' crossing, with some 75 or 80 new colonists and fresh supplies (there should have been more, but an accompanying vessel had been lost in heavy fog), commanded by Captain – and Councillor – Christopher Newport. To his dismay, he found only 38 survivors, two councillors dead (Gosnold and Kendall), two weak from illness (Ratcliffe and Martin), one under arrest (Wingfield), one under sentence of death (Smith), and a wholly new, irregular councillor, Archer, apparently running the show. He immediately took charge: in no time the absurd charges against Smith were dismissed, Wingfield was released from the pinnace – but not reinstated – and Archer dismissed from the council (but kept on as Recorder, or secretary); in addition, a new councillor, Matthew Scrivener, linked by marriage to Wingfield, and a major investor and, consequently, appointed on the Company's order, was installed. Now Smith's new little friend, Pocahontas, appeared on the scene, with offerings of food from Powhatan for his new 'son' and the new great white chief, whom Smith had described in glowing terms. With the new year, it seemed time to start again.

Gilded Dirt

Before the colonists could go forward, there was an almost immediate setback. Within a few days of the newcomers' landing, one of them accidentally caused a fire in the fort, and, despite the desperate efforts to control it, all but three of the flimsy buildings were destroyed, including the little church; Smith admired the stoicism of Revd Hunt, who 'lost all his library and all he had but the clothes on his back, yet none never heard him repine at his loss'. Fortunately, a lot of the provisions on board the *John and Francis* had not been unloaded. What also kept them going was food supplies – venison, raccoons, bread – from Powhatan, sent to demonstrate his munificence to the new English werowance, and delivered every few days by Pocahontas, who 'with her attendants ... saved many of their lives, that else for all this had starved with hunger'. What did not please Smith, however, was the excessively generous payment the new commander and colonists were giving for this food. A rapid inflation set in: 'In a short time it followed, that could not be had for a pound of copper, which before was sold for an ounce', wrote Anas Todkill, John Martin's servant. Newport would have heard Smith's account of the great chief, Powhatan, and thought it advantageous to please and impress his opposite number.

The next few weeks were occupied with reconstruction and settling in. Agreement was reached with the werowance of the Paspeheghs to look for Roanoke survivors in the village of Panawaioc, nearly 150 miles away; however, Wowinchopunck merely took the Englishmen 20 miles downstream, stayed a few days, and brought them back, 'deluding us for rewards', as Smith wrote. Probably Wowinchopunck knew it would be a waste of effort; in any case, no further attempt was made.

In February, Powhatan sent a message that he would be pleased to receive Smith's great father, an opportunity that Newport jumped at. In England, he had told Lord Salisbury that Virginia was 'excellent and very rich in gold and copper', and had brought samples with him to be assayed. On the strength of this, on 12 August, Sir Walter Cope had written excitedly to his Lordship that 'we are fallen upon a land that promises more than the land of promise: instead of milk we find pearl, and gold instead of honey': with so much gold in the offing, perhaps potential investors in the East India Company might be persuaded to transfer their money. The next day, after the samples had been properly assayed, he wrote that, like an alchemist's experiment, 'all had turned to vapour', that Virginia was 'more like to prove the land of Canaan than the land of Ophir [fabled for gold]', and angrily accused John Martin of deception. Sir Thomas Smythe had to reassure Salisbury that Newport had resolved 'never to see your Lordship before he bring that with him which he confidently believed he had brought before'. A new venture was hurriedly fitted out; among those taken, apart from the usual gentle-men adventurers, were two gold refiners, two goldsmiths and a jeweller (as well as more useful characters such as a surgeon, two apothecaries and a gunner). Newport's reputation was at stake: now he needed to find gold – and if there was any gold in the area, surely Powhatan would know where it was.

So, with plenty of presents and about 40 armed men, Newport, Smith and Scrivener set off in the barge and the pinnace, down the James River and around the corner to Powhatan's capital of Werocomoco, one mile inland from the York/Pamunkey River. Once there, despite an enthusi-astic reception party, Newport kept his state on board the pinnace, with Scrivener, while Smith went ashore with 20 men wearing 'jacks', quilted leather jerkins reinforced with metal plates, thought to be arrow-proof. Halfway to the village was a frail, narrow bridge, difficult to cross; Smith, ever cautious, sent his men over half at a time, with the other half on guard. At the longhouse, that Smith would have remembered vividly, Powhatan gave him a warm welcome, with 40 or more platters of bread set out, and a large crowd of wives, concubines and warriors in attendance, and bearing himself 'with such majesty as I cannot express, nor yet have often seen either in pagan or Christian'. Smith presented him with Newport's gifts: a coat of red cloth, a white greyhound dog (much appreciated) and a 'sugar-loaf' hat (high London fashion). Three of Powhatan's 'nobles' accepted the gifts with 'a great oration' and promises of friendship. There was a banquet, with Smith once again served by the werowansquaw of Appomattoc – this time he called her 'a comely young savage'. Powhatan then said how pleased he was to see Smith, and asked after Newport (who had upstaged him by his absence), and was assured that he would come the next day. The verbal fencing then began, as at their first meeting.

Powhatan began by asking, 'with a merry countenance', where were the cannon that Smith had promised; Smith replied that he had offered the men the two cannon, 'but they refused to take them'. At that, Powhatan laughed, and asked Smith to give him some that were not so heavy. He then asked about Smith's men, waiting outside, and said that he would be pleased to receive them, inside. Smith agreed, and told his men to go in, not all together, but only two at a time, which was safer for everybody. Each pair was then presented to the great chief, and given four or five pounds of bread. After this ceremony, Powhatan said that they should all lay down their weapons before him, as a sign of respect for his authority, but Smith politely refused: 'I told him that was a ceremony our enemies desired, but never our friends.' For all that, he should know that the English were his friends, and that the next day Newport would give him one of his 'sons', and furthermore would be willing to help him by conquering the tribes he had said were his enemies – the Monacans to the west and the Susquehannocks to the north – delivering them to his

John Smith's portrait engraved by Simon Van de Passe as it appeared in his
Description of New England in June, 1616. At top left are pikemen (from his
Netherlands time), at top right the globe and compasses indicate an explorer
and mapmaker, at bottom right a captain rides his horse, and at bottom left a
ship crosses the Atlantic.

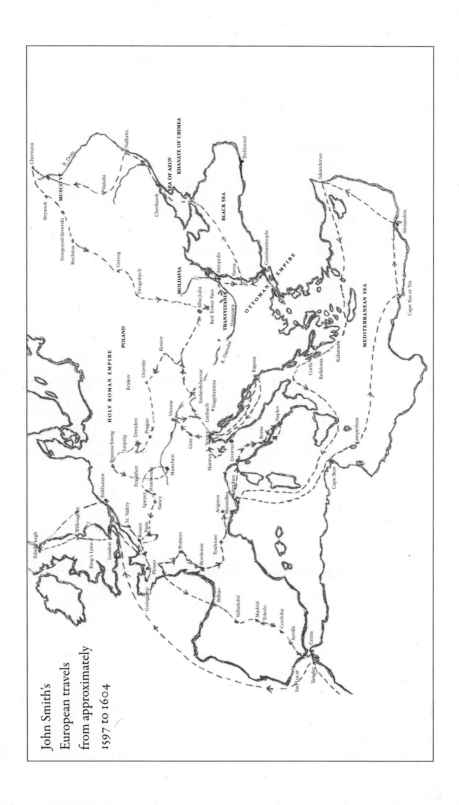

John Smith's
European travels
from approximately
1597 to 1604

A gentleman posing with an arquebus (a musket on a rest). In battle he would have worn a helmet, at least.

A Turkish delli, a horsemen armed with scimitar and spear, wearing animal skins, with eagles' wings attached to his shield.

A Turkish janissary, with scimitar, musket and firecracker, wearing a white felt cap with long plumes as a decoration for bravery.

Smith's first joust against the Turks, piercing his opponent's visor.

Smith's second joust. Both men's lances have shattered and Smith's pistol shot has wounded and unhorsed his opponent.

Smith's final joust. He lost his battle-axe, but pierced his opponent's back armour with his falchion.

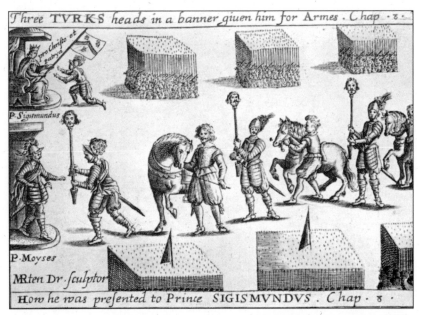

How he was presented to Prince SIGISMVNDVS . Chap · 8 ·

After his three jousts, Smith was presented to his general, Moses Székely (not to Prince Sigismund) who embraced and rewarded him.

Constantinople where Smith met his admirer, Trabigzanda, is depicted with the Sultan's palace in the foreground, An engraving by Georg Braun c. 1600.

A Greek or Turkish girl, drawn by John White. She wears a gold necklace and bracelet, and carries a rose and a pomegranate (with romantic associations).

The appearance of the *Susan Constant*, the smaller *God Speed* and the little pinnace, *Discovery*, off Virginia in 1607.

Smith's map of Virginia, specifically the Chesapeake Bay area, with west at the top, engraved by William Hole. On the right is a 'giant-like' Susquehannock warrior, and top left Powhatan is shown in his longhouse when he first met Smith.

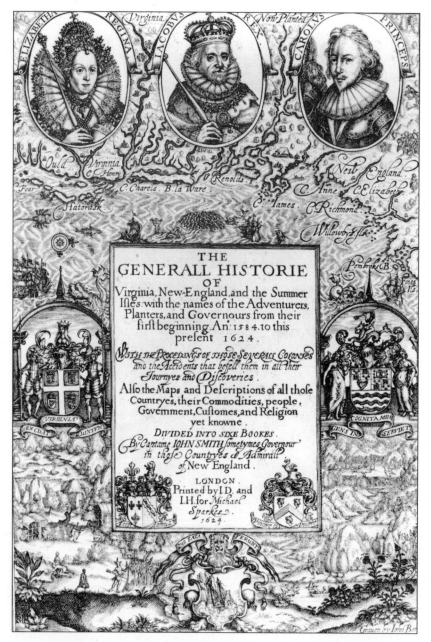

The title page of Smith's '*Generall Historie*'. His coat of arms is shown in the central tablet. Above, Queen Elizabeth, King James and Prnce Charles dominate East Virginia, with place-names chosen by Prince Charles.

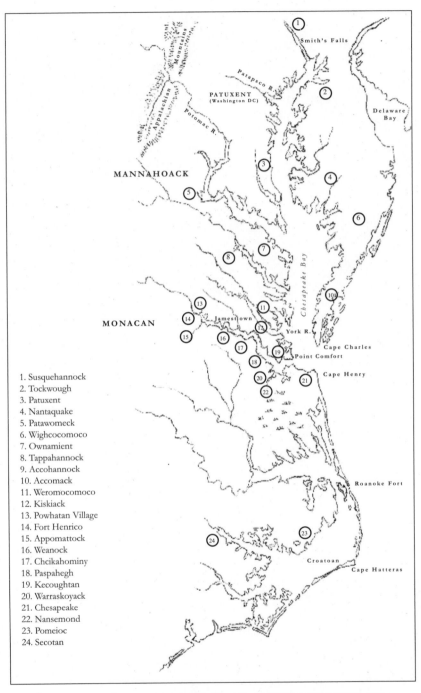

The Indian tribes of East Virginia. Powhatan's empire stretched from the Patuxents in the north to the Nansemonds in the south.

Preparing a log boat, probably from a tulip tree or white cypress. The tree was felled by burning the base and the trunk hollowed by burning and scraping with shells.

Smith's initial examination by Indian priests

Indians fishing. A picture by Theodor de Bry, based on a John White drawing. In the water are stingrays, king crabs, sturgeon, catfish, a loggerhead turtle and a hammerhead shark. The little fire in the canoe was used at night, to attract fish. A fish weir is shown on the left.

Indian woman and girl playing with a European doll; adapted by Theodor de Bry from John White.

Pomeioc village by de Bry, based on John White.
A (bottom Left) contained dead kings' remains; B was a sacred place for
prayers; at C villagers danced and celebrated; at D they set up feasts, whilst K
was for more solemn occasions. At E (left) tobacco is growing, F (with a bird-
scarer), G, H are maize fields; pumpkins grow at L.

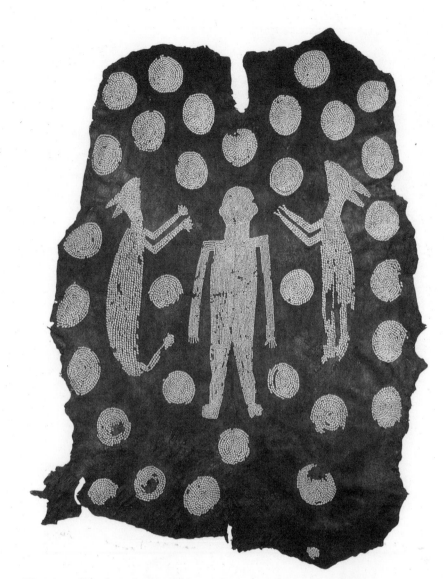

Known as 'Powhatan's Mantle', part of John Tradescant's collection, now in the Ashmolean Museum, Oxford. The discs may represent villages.

C. Smith taketh the King of Pamavnkee prisoner 1608

The Countrey wee now call Virginia beginneth at Cape Henry distant
from Roanoack 60 miles, where was S.ʳ Walter Raleigh's plantation:
and because the people differ very little from them of Powhatan in any
thing, I have inserted those figures in this place because of the conveniency.

Smith's defeat of the Indian Chief, Opechancanough, as depicted in his *Generall Historie*. Note the height disparity between the two men.

Portrait of Pocahontas by Simon Van de Passe, on her visit to England in 1616, giving her true native name – Matoaka – and her English name of Rebecca Rolfe.

Lady Frances, Countess of Hertford, Smith's patron for the '*Generall Historie*', shown in her youth before they met.

'subjection'. Powhatan responded with a 'loud oration' to the assembled company, proclaiming Smith a werowance (again) and that 'the corn, women and country' would belong to the English as much as to his own people (Smith may not have passed this on to his men, most of whom had been underfed and unwillingly celibate for some time). Unusually, Powhatan then courteously rose from his mats and escorted him from the longhouse.

When they reached the river, however, it was to find that the tide was out, leaving the barge stuck inaccessibly in the mud. Rain began to fall; Powhatan graciously allowed Smith and his men to stay the night in another longhouse, stored with bows and arrows. Smith arranged that two men should guard each entrance all night, whilst he was invited back by Powhatan for another meal (the bulk of it sent over to Smith's men), where they spent several hours in what Smith variously called 'ancient' or 'pretty discourses to renew their old acquaintance', whatever that means – probably the usual mutual misinformation and bragging.

The next morning, Powhatan came and escorted him to the river, pointing out the large number of canoes on the banks and explaining how they were sent out to collect tribute from his many subjects. This metaphorical blowing of his own trumpet was countered by several loud, braying calls from a real trumpet, announcing with sensational effect the approach of Captain Newport. In the longhouse, Powhatan welcomed Newport graciously; in turn, Newport, in token of friendship, presented him with a 13-year-old 'son', a boy whose name, Thomas Savage, had probably got him the job of training as interpreter and go-between. Such hostage exchanges were not uncommon at the time. Young Savage may well have gone willingly to take his chance: that he had joined the expedition at all showed a venturesome spirit comparable to that of young John Smith; he survived, and eventually did well. Powhatan later reciprocated by sending a young man named Namontack, who had already acted as a guide, described by the wary Smith as Powhatan's 'trusty servant and one of a shrewd and subtle capacity', sent 'to know our strength and country's condition'.

At a welcoming breakfast, Powhatan attempted a previous ploy: why had the English brought their weapons, since he was their friend and had not brought weapons to the meal? Smith, speaking on Newport's behalf, replied that it was merely the custom of their people, not an unfriendly gesture. Newport, however, seeking to impress, over-ruled him – no doubt to Smith's horror – and sent the rest of the men away to the waterside (though Smith ensured that there was always a guard on the barge, giving them access to the *Discovery* out in the river, and that either he or Scrivener was always with Newport). Now it was time to trade, hatchets and copper pots for corn and venison. Smith had always traded piecemeal, bargaining for items one by one. Powhatan, sensing from Newport's previous behaviour the nature of the man he had to deal with, now grandly declared, 'Captain Newport, it is not agreeable with my greatness, in this peddling manner to trade for trifles, and I esteem you a great werowance. Therefore lay me down all your commodities together. What I like I will take, and in recompence give you that I think fitting their value.'

One would have thought that anyone would have seen through this, especially with Smith urging against agreement, but not Newport, still eager to display his magnificence and 'ostentation of greatness', as Todkill put it. So copper pots and iron hatchets, for which Smith had expected the equivalent of some 20 hogsheads (large barrels of 60 to 70 gallons each), went for only four bushels (eight gallons each). 'This bred some unkindness between our two captains [formerly on good terms, but now increasingly distant], Newport seeking to please the humour of the insatiable savage', and so get him to reveal where gold might be found, Smith bargaining 'to cause the savage to please him', and sell him enough food to get the colony through the winter.

To rescue the situation, Smith began ostentatiously toying with some blue beads, probably Venetian glass from the latest shipment. Powhatan was immediately taken with them, but Smith put him off: the beads were, he explained, 'composed of a most rare substance of the colour of the skies, and not to be worn but by the greatest kings in the world.

This made him half mad to be the owner of such strange jewels.' Powhatan offered two pecks of corn, but, it being a seller's market, had to pay three (a peck is a quarter of a bushel). The next day, for a few more of the beads, he paid two bushels. He also sent plenty of venison and more bushels of corn.

During the next few days' trading, negotiating and diplomatic partying, the winter rains became even worse, the area around becoming increasingly marshy, with the barge having difficulty with the rising and variably tidal river. On one occasion, Smith was 'pestered in the ooze', that is, stuck in the mud: the Indians offered to wade in and carry him out on their heads, but he refused, asking only for firewood and mats as cover to be brought out, which they did with 'pains a horse would scarce have endured, yet a couple of bells richly contented them'. Later, a senior Indian carried out food, taking pride in stoically enduring 'that miserable, cold and dirty passage, though a dog would scarce have endured it [a favourite phrase]'. This kindness to their guests, he noted, he 'found when I little expected less than a mischief, but the black night parting our companies, ere midnight the flood [tide] served to carry us aboard [*Discovery*]'.

In the next day's negotiations, Powhatan brought up the English offer to help him against his enemies; contradicting what he had said earlier, he now said that the Monacans were not his absolute enemies, but that he was willing to help the English attack them. He and Newport, 'being great werowances' (he had realised the power of flattery over Newport), should not take part in person, but Smith and Scrivener could go with Opechancanough and 100 braves – and 100 or 150 Englishmen (almost their entire strength) should be enough; all he asked was that the women and children (the usual object of Indian warfare, as Strachey noted) should be spared and given to him. Newport was quite keen, thinking that the expeditionary force might 'undertake by this means to discover the South Sea', but Smith's suspicions prevented this unlikely enterprise. The Englishmen, wandering far away in strange woods with a large force of braves, could easily be chopped up, while Jamestown would have been practically defenceless – but Newport had not thought of that.

Shortly after this, Opechancanough sent messages inviting Newport and Smith to visit him at his village, which Powhatan tried to discourage (probably trying for a trading monopoly), but eventually they went, about a dozen miles upstream. After their first meeting in the woods, Opechancanough now greeted Smith (in theory, his adopted kinsman) 'with a natural kind affection; he seemed to rejoice to see me'. This visit, and the next to a nearby village, Menacapant, were marked by feasting, 'playing, dancing and delight', and mutually satisfying trading, Newport – or, rather, Smith – eventually leaving with some 250 bushels of grain, enough to last them until the next supply ship. Leaving Smith behind in the barge 'to dig a rock', as Smith dismissively phrased it, hoping for gold ore, Newport went off in the pinnace, arriving in Jamestown on 9 March, according to Wingfield, 'well laden with corn, wheat, beans and peas, to our great comfort and his worthy commendations' – not that Wingfield would ever have commended yeoman Smith, whilst Newport was far more concerned to find the gold he had promised to provide his masters in England.

A gold-fever now set in, driven by Newport and supported by Ratcliffe, Archer and John Martin, the goldsmith's son. 'Both Scrivener and Smith did their best to amend what was amiss,' wrote Todkill, 'but with the President went the major part, [so] that their horns were too short. But the worst mischief was, our gilded refiners with their golden promises made all men their slaves in hope of recompence: there was no talk, no hope, no work, but dig gold, wash gold, refine gold, load gold' – though, ironically, once again, none of it was indeed gold.

Smith, of course, was disgusted, rightly incredulous of the results of their assaying, angry 'to see all necessary business neglected, to fraught such a drunken ship with so much gilded dirt'. In his view, Newport and his men could 'well have been gone in 14 days', instead of staying and consuming the supplies of pork, beef, oil, cheese and beer intended for the colonists, while the crew of 'this removing tavern' sold their own foodstuffs to wealthier colonists 'at 15 times the value'.

Amidst all this annoyance and frustration, Smith had at least one little pleasure, the continuing visits from young Pocahontas: 'very oft she came to our fort, with what she could get for Captain Smith'. William Strachey recalled her as 'a well-featured but wanton [playful] young girl ... of the age then of 11 or 12 years', who would play with the boys in the fort market-place, 'and make them [cart-]wheel, falling on their hands, turning their heads upwards, whom she would follow, and wheel so, herself naked as she was, all the fort over' (it was not until puberty that Indian girls wore a sort of leather apron and became 'very shamefaced to be seen bare'). An intelligent, lively child, she was clearly intrigued by Smith and the English, who probably took more of an interest in her than did her own people. Smith would have chatted with her, improving his Algonquian and knowledge of the people, and taken a kindly, avuncular interest. In his *Map of Virginia* of 1612, in his list of Indian words and sentences, he included, 'Kekaten pokahontas patiaquagh ningh tanks manotyens neer mowchick rawrenock andowgh', translated as, 'Bid Pocahontas bring hither two little baskets and I will give her white beads to make her a chain.' (It should not be assumed that he expected her baskets to be empty.)

At last, on Sunday 10 April, after nearly three and a half months, everything was ready for Newport's return home. The gilded dirt was loaded up and a few passengers on board – Powhatan's agent Namontack bravely venturing alone far from his homeland, and a mysterious person, thought to be Irish, named Francis Maguel or Magner, who sold some information to the Spanish in 1610, and two others. The colony not having any need for 'Parliaments ... petitions, admirals, recorders, interpreters, chronologers, courts of plea, nor justices of the peace', as Todkill wrote, they 'sent Master Wingfield and Captain Archer with him for England, to seek some better place of employment'. Wingfield had to go as failed leader, whilst Archer had to be sent back, partly for his own safety, as an ambitious troublemaker, one 'whose insolency did look upon that little, himself, with great-sighted [magnifying] spectacles, derogating from others' merits by spewing out his venomous libels', in Wingfield's words. They would be only a few feet away from each other, on board, for nearly six weeks. Smith may well have thought that the air had cleared in Jamestown – but Wingfield, Archer and Newport would soon be back at headquarters in London, ready and eager to tell the ruling Council their version of events.

9

The *Phoenix* and the Nonpareil

Smith and Scrivener saw Newport off, accompanying him in the barge as far as Cape Henry; after the last shouted farewells, the ship put on sail and made off eastward towards the open sea and England, while the barge turned south, down to the mouth of the James River, to the territory of the Nansemond people. This was a powerful tribe of some 200 fighting men, semi-independent of Powhatan. The English held them responsible for the initial attack upon them in 1607, and Newport had carried out a reprisal attack on his return in 1608, when 'some of them enticing him to their ambuscadoes by a dance, he perceiving [or mistaking?] their intent, with a volley of musket-shot slew one, and shot one or two more.' A cautious approach was advisable; a messenger came out in a canoe, inviting them to land, which, after some shilly-shallying and negotiation, they did, spending the night in a village a little way up the Nansemond River, at that point 'a musket shot broad', and then trading. The land, Smith wrote, contained a '1000 acres of most excellent fertile ground, so sweet, so pleasant, so beautiful, and so strong a prospect for an invincible strong city, with so many commodities, that I know as yet I have not seen.' He thought he was probably within a day's journey of Chawanoac, where in 1585–6, Ralph Lane, commander of the Roanoke colony, had directed a group of colonists to live among Indians and a 'multitude of bears', but there was no word of the lost people.

Then it was back to Jamestown, and rebuilding the neglected township and dealing with fresh trouble from the natives, grown confident from familiarity and the departure of Captain Newport's cannon. Powhatan had sent him a farewell present of 20 turkeys, in expectation of a reciprocal courtesy gift – of 20 swords. Perhaps predictably, Newport, never the sharpest sword in the armoury, sent the most dangerous Indian chief in the area 20 swords. Now Powhatan tried to repeat the ploy, sending young Thomas Savage to Smith with more turkeys, with a request for a similar return. Smith promptly gave the Indians little presents, and Powhatan a blunt refusal. This was the cue for the Indians to try to steal iron tools or swords, even brazenly snatching them from men's hands, with Opechancanough operating as chief receiver of stolen property. One man having tried to steal two swords, Smith got the Council's permission to put him in the 'bilboes' (like metal stocks) for the day. The next day the man came back with three more, armed with wooden swords; when Smith told them to be off, they would not, and the leader attempted to strike him, but Smith, never slow to react, struck first. The rest came at him, but were very quickly beaten 'up and down the isle' and off, with a few musket-shots to speed them on their way. This vigorous reaction brought an appropriate response, with pleas for friendship and offers to help work on the fishing weirs set up near the camp. Word got around, and the chief of the Nansemonds even sent over a hatchet that had been stolen at the last visit.

On Wednesday 20 April, as men were at work chopping trees, the alarm was sounded, causing them to snatch up their weapons to resist the long-expected Spanish attack. Instead, the new ship flew the English flag: it was the *Phoenix*, commanded by Captain Thomas Nelson, that had set out with Newport the previous October, got separated when within sight of America, been driven south by 'extreme storms and tempests', wintered in the West Indies, and at last, despite contrary winds, carried out orders and come to join them, and so 'ravish [them] with exceeding joy'. Furthermore, despite the long journey, Nelson had conscientiously seen to it that the colonists' supplies had not been broached.

Some 60 or more new colonists now strengthened their numbers, whose muscles and skills would be very welcome. 'Now we thought ourselves as well fitted as our hearts could wish,' Smith recalled.

With these reinforcements, more vigorous exploration could be undertaken, and it was agreed that Smith and Scrivener (partly to keep them out of the gold-grubbers' hair) should lead 70 colonists and crewmen from the *Phoenix* up beyond the falls of the James River. The men spent a week being trained by Smith in marching and how to fight and skirmish in the woods, and resist the anticipated Indian guerilla warfare, until they felt themselves fully confident and competent. However, Captain Nelson went by the book: his sailors could not go unless the company guaranteed to pay their extra wages and compensate the ship for lost time. Plenty was said; but nothing could be done. So, instead, 50 men settled for planting corn and other vegetables and chopping trees for timber, for eventual sale in England, and another 80 or so remained 'to do the command of the President and Captain Martin' – gold-grubbing again. The ship's return was delayed, while the timber export versus gold-sample dispute went on.

Meanwhile, the natives' tool- and weapon-stealing was getting out of hand. In early May, an Indian who had stolen an axe was pursued by Scrivener and others, and threatened his pursuers with bow and arrow. A few days later, when Smith and Scrivener were out in the cornfield, two painted Indians armed with cudgels came circling about them, 'as though they would have clubbed me like a hare'; the Englishmen withdrew into the fort. More Indians arrived, with stories of wanting to come into the fort to punish one of their men in there (Amocis, a sort of resident spy), then more entered and attempted to attack Smith. They promptly found themselves shut in, and 'apprehended', as he phrased it. The rest of the council agreed on action, seized and imprisoned eight more Indians, and decided to wait and see. An hour later, some unfamiliar warriors, 'extraordinarily fitted with arrows, skins and shooting gloves' (the heavy mob), arrived outside the fort and hung about for a while in a threatening manner. The English waited. The following day, messengers were twice sent to speak to Smith, who were told to bring back the swords, spades, shovels and other tools that had been stolen, or the prisoners, now numbering about 16, would be hanged the next day. The next message was that the Indians had captured two colonists in the wood: unless the prisoners were released, these two would hang. That night, Smith got the approval of Ratcliffe and Martin to lead out a party in the barge on a raiding mission, burning villages and canoes (huts could quickly be replaced, but dugout canoes took days to make, by burning and chiselling with mussel shells). The two Englishmen were released.

The council now released one Indian prisoner, as a token of good intent. The rest were brought, twice a day, well guarded, to morning and evening prayer, among Englishmen in full armour, a confrontation with an alien god and ritual they found unnerving in the extreme. The council then instructed Smith to 'terrify them with some torture', to find out what was intended. Unlike normal contemporary practice in Europe among the English, Spanish and others – and, notoriously, now some modern countries – the torture was limited and only psychological, not physical. One man was tied to the mainmast of the pinnace, with six men aiming primed muskets at him; he had been trained to endure pain, but this was different. He could not answer Smith's questions, but knew a man who could, called Macanoe.

Macanoe was taken aside and terrified in his turn, first with the sight of the rack, the effect of which could be guessed (who could have thought to transport such a monstrosity across the Atlantic?), 'then with muskets, which seeing, he desired me to stay', and confessed Powhatan's plan. The Chickahominy, Youghtanund, Pamunkey, Mattapanient and Kiskiack tribes were 'altogether a-hunting' for them. The Paspahegh and Chickahominies intended to surprise them at work, and seize their tools that way. Powhatan was going to profess friendship until Newport returned with his man Namontack, and then, 'with a great feast he would so enamour Captain Newport and his men, as they should seize on him, and the like traps would be set for the rest'.

Now Smith sent young Savage back to Powhatan, with a message to the effect that the English only wanted peace, and to come to Werocomoco village to find stones suitable for making hatchets like the Indians' tomahawks (a bizarre suggestion); but if the Indians so much as fired one arrow at them, they would 'destroy' them. He concluded with a request for an Indian named Weanock as a guide. Powhatan countered by returning young Savage with his box and clothes, and asking for a different boy; Savage had indeed suspected that something was going on. Smith in turn sent no replacement, but 'many messages and presents'; Powhatan sent Weanock as requested, and said he would accept Savage; Smith did not send him. Stalemate. Then Weanock ran off, and some Paspaheghs arrived, again wanting Amocis. Smith needed to find out what was going on.

He and Scrivener then divided their captives into separate groups, and had volleys of shots fired in their hearing, causing each group to think that the others had been shot. Thus terrorised, they confirmed Macanoe's story, that the Paspaheghs and Chickahominies were determined to attack them, revealed who had taken the swords and that Powhatan had received them (until then, Martin had been prepared to believe Powhatan).

Word of the detention of his braves had reached Powhatan, who now, as Smith put it in his *True Relation*, 'sent his daughter, a child of ten years old, which not only for feature, countenance and proportion much exceedeth any of the rest of his people, but for wit and spirit, the only Nonpariel [*sic*: nonpareil; unequalled paragon] of his country.' This is the first reference to her in that mangled text, but she was almost certainly mentioned before in an excised passage. The charming young princess was accompanied, in an almost fairy-tale pairing, by his old acquaintance Rawhunt, 'as much exceeding in deformity of person, but of a subtle wit and crafty understanding'. Rawhunt then told Smith how much Powhatan 'loved and respected' him (the latter, possibly), how he had sent his daughter with presents of venison and bread, and asking for Thomas Savage, whom also he now 'loved exceedingly'. Pocahontas took no part in negotiations, but awaited the arrival of the prisoners' fathers and friends. Even Opechancanough got involved on behalf of two of his men, sending as token of submission his shooting glove and arm-brace.

This looked much like victory; in response to all this, the council yielded, first marching the prisoners along for another fearsome dose of Christian worship, before feeding them, returning their bows and arrows and handing them over to young Pocahontas, who was also 'requited with such trifles as contented her'. There was a last, brief scare of another ambush the next day, but everything seemed to have settled down.

Two days later, an Indian came to Jamestown to show them 'a glistering mineral stone', such as the Indians gathered that the English were, for some reason, interested in. Smith was sent off with a dozen men, to investigate, but soon began to suspect that the man was deliberately misleading them, and called a halt. He showed the man the pieces of copper he had intended to give him if he had led them properly; this angered the man, who became abusive, for which he got 20 lashes with a rope, and sent off with a challenge to fire an arrow if he dared. That, for a while, was the end of Indian adventures; all was quiet on the western front.

Now it was getting more than time for Nelson to be off, before he started charging for unnecessary delay. The ship was loaded with a good stock of profitable red cedarwood as its main cargo (a victory for Smith). With it went some mineral samples, what Smith called Martin's 'fantastical gold', and, with that, John Martin himself, who had 'made shift to be sick near a year', and who, 'desirous to enjoy the credit of his supposed art of finding the golden mine, was most willingly admitted to return for England', as his distinctly unimpressed servant, Anas Todkill, wrote, who elected to stay on in Virginia. With the ship also went the document eventually published in 1608, in edited and probably censored form, as the *True Relation of such occurrences and accidents of noate as hath happened in Virginia since the first planting of that Colony ... .* Written by Smith, ostensibly as a lengthy, private letter of over 13,000 words to an unknown 'worshipful friend', it was a report, very much from his own point of view, of the happenings during the Virginia venture, from the foul weather of December 1606, through the various disputes, successes and misfortunes to the end of May of that year. Smith, or the editor, concluded with some PR flannel about the colonists all being 'well contented, free from mutinies, in love with one another, and as we hope in continual peace with the Indians'. John Martin, however, would be in England, with his own story.

Smith also sent a map of the region north of the River James, based on what he had seen and what the natives had told him, intended for Henry Hudson. On Thursday, 2 June, the *Phoenix* was released from her moorings and slipped downriver into the morning light, leaving behind 100–150 men, 'very bare,' wrote George Percy, 'and scanty of victuals, furthermore in wars and in danger of the savages'. For all that, there was work to be done. Leaving Ratcliffe and Scrivener (as an inadequate brake on the *folies de grandeur* of the President), Smith prepared for further exploration in the barge, sailing with Nelson out as far as Cape Henry, where the muddy river waters merged with the choppy waves of the great bay. There, and not before, he handed over his papers to Captain Nelson: they should now be safe, and come to the right hands. He was not to know of the flutter they would cause in London.

10

Trips Round the Bay

Hoping that the colonists were now sufficiently at peace with the natives and 'in love with one another', Smith now set off on another voyage of exploration, northwards through Chesapeake Bay, in hope of a breakthrough to the other sea. With him in the open sailing-barge or galliot he took 14 men, including six gentlemen, Walter Russell, a newcomer and 'doctor of physic', Anas Todkill, now one of Smith's supporters, James Read the blacksmith, who had been involved in the fracas with Ratcliffe and was as well kept out of the way, a fisherman, a fish-monger and three 'soldiers'. They crossed the mouth of the bay, past Cape Charles and its low, neighbouring islands (now called Smith Island), and sailed northwards up the eastern side of the bay.

Soon they encountered two 'grim and stout savages' in a canoe, equipped with long poles like javelins, tipped with bone, for spearing fish, who were at first distinctly confrontational – being from the other side of the bay they were not subject to Powhatan, and knew nothing of the English – but eventually guided the explorers to their village of Accomac. Here the werowance ('the comeliest, proper, civil savage we encountered') told Smith a strange story: after the death of two village children, their parents went to see the bodies laid out on platforms to decompose, only to find them in apparently excellent condition, with 'delightful countenances, as though they had regained their vital spirits'.

Many people came to view this 'miracle', but all who did very soon died, and the surviving remnant were now in mourning.

After this unsettling narration – perhaps intended to discourage lingering – they went on up the western coast of the peninsula, inspecting and mapping the many inlets and bays, with a view to possible future harbours and settlements. Caught in a sudden, violent storm, 'that with great danger we escaped the unmerciful raging of that ocean-like water', and looking for fresh water, they went up a promising-looking channel only to encounter an initially hostile crowd of Indians, who then changed and welcomed them with 'songs, dances and much mirth', but could provide only three casks of almost undrinkable water. Their own stocks were nearly exhausted; soon, he wrote, 'we would have refused two barricoes [kegs] of gold for one of that puddle water'. Eventually they found a large pond of fresh, but strangely hot, water that they could use for drinking. Smith named the place Point Ployer, in honour of the Comte de Plouër, who had helped him in Brittany eight eventful years earlier. Shortly after this, they were struck by another violent storm of wind and rain, that smashed their mast and nearly sank them, but after some desperate baling they were able to shelter on a small, empty island. Stuck there for two days, they set to, to replace the mast and repair the sail with their shirts, cobbled together. They named the island Limbo, after the nowhere, no-time place where Dante put unbaptised souls.

Pushing on, they entered another river mouth and met yet more hostile, if rather small, Indians, who ran about 'as amazed', some of them climbing into the treetops to shower them with arrows, and showing 'the greatest passion they could express of their anger' (as Russell and Todkill wrote in *Proceedings of the English Colonie*, in *A Map of Virginia*). The explorers did not retaliate, but anchored offshore, out of range. The next morning the tribesmen came down to the shore and danced in a ring, carrying closed baskets suggestive of gifts or trade goods. Smith nevertheless decided that this was a trap, and had his men fire a volley of pistol-shot from their muskets, to frighten rather than harm. The villagers fled, scattering into the reedbeds nearby. That evening, after another volley of shot to clear the way, Smith led his men ashore, to find only a few deserted huts with abandoned cooking fires; they left some pieces of copper, bells and little mirrors. In the morning, four men paddled up in a canoe, who said that they had been away fishing, and knew nothing of the previous unpleasantness. These people, the Nantaquakes, were beyond Powhatan's empire, and even spoke a different language, but one sufficiently alike for Smith to understand the gist. He treated them 'with courtesy' and gave them some small presents; the men then went ashore, returning shortly afterwards with a score or so more, now friendly. Soon there was a large crowd of men, women and children, all friendly, happy to receive beads and to trade ('the best merchants of all other savages') and provide information – in translation – about the neighbours, particularly an aggressive and fearsome tribe, the Massawomekes, who Smith immediately became keen to encounter.

They sailed ever northward, now hugging the mainland side of the bay, passing a high point that Smith named Rickards Cliffs, in memory of his mother's family, then past land apparently empty of people but heavily wooded, 'full of wolves, bears, deer and other wild beasts'. The monotonous silence and (human) emptiness of the unending primeval forest began to prey on the men's nerves – that, the labour of rowing the barge when they could not sail, and their damp, increasingly mouldy bread. Demands to return to Jamestown began to be heard.

To rally his dispirited troops, Smith countered with a speech derived from his reading in Hakluyt's *Voyages*, reminding them of how Sir Ralph Lane's men, some 20 years earlier, in similar circumstances had pressed on, willing to survive on guide dog boiled with sassafras leaves (not that his men had any dogs). He assured them that he would share in all their tribulations, and diet. They should not fear being lost 'in these unknown large waters, or ... being swallowed up in some strong gust: abandon those childish fears,' he urged them, 'for worse than is past cannot happen' – surely just asking for trouble – 'and there is as much danger to return as to proceed forward'. Excelsior, or words to that effect. How comforting and inspiring they found this is doubtful, especially when he insisted that he would not go back until he had seen the Massawomekes and 'Patawomeck, the head of this great water'.

So a little further north they went, but the weather was against them; some men fell ill, and Smith had to turn back. By 16 June they were at the mouth of the Potomac River. 'Fear being gone, and our men recovered, we were all contented to take some pains to know the name of this nine-mile broad river'; there still did not seem to be any people about. At last, after about 30 miles, they met two men in a canoe, who led them 'up a little bayed creek towards Onawmient' on the south bank, where they soon found themselves confronted by several hundred Indians, 'so strangely painted, grimed and disguised, shouting, yelling and crying, as [that] so many spirits from Hell could not have showed more terrible'. Unperturbed, Smith characteristically responded by firing at them with such 'seeming willingness', the bullets however only bouncing and splashing on the surface of the water, which, with the thunderous echo resounding from the surrounding wood 'so amazed them, as [that] down went their bows and arrows', they treated for peace, and the two sides exchanged hostages.

At this place, Smith was told by the tribesmen that they had been instructed to attack them by Powhatan, himself encouraged by some 'discontents' in Jamestown, because 'our captain did cause them to stay in the country against their wills'. He does not expand on this in his *Generall Historie*, but it seems likely that, what with the discomfort, debility and death rate in Jamestown, not a few men had grumbled to Indians that they would have cleared off long ago if it had not been for that pigheaded Captain Smith.

Undeterred, the explorers went farther up the Potomac, now identified as the River Patawomeck that he had been set on finding. On the way, they picked up an Indian named Mosco, unusual in having a thick, bushy beard, suggestive of European, probably French, ancestry, who was pleased to go along with this equally hairy captain and crew, as a guide and general helper. With him they went far upriver, past the site of modern Washington, D.C. (then undistinguishable from the general mud and woodland), looking for the place where an Indian had told Newport that he had seen some 'glistering metal'. At last, they found some rocky cliffs, below which the stream had left a 'tinctured, spangled scurf, that made many places seem as gilded', with the earth sprinkled with 'yellow spangles as if it had been pin-dust' (dust from grinding brass pins). The werowance of Patawomeck village, a little downstream, told Smith he might find more at a nearby creek, so he took six men and some guides back up, chaining the Indians to himself and his men to ensure that they could not abandon them, but promising to give them the chains when they returned, which seemed to please them.

They found a sort of mine, a pit that had been dug with shells and hatchets, with a stream used for sifting out the ore, which the Indian miners used to 'put in little bags and sell it all over the country to paint their bodies, faces or idols; which makes them look like blackamoors dusted over with silver'. Smith's men gathered up as much as they could manage and loaded it onto the barge to transfer to Jamestown. Predictably, nothing came of it.

On the other hand, more obviously profitable in the short term, as furs, were the numerous otters, beavers, martens, lynx and mink, as well as, of more immediate interest, the multitude of fish in the river, 'lying so thick with their heads above the water [was the stream low, or deoxygenated?], as for want of nets (our boat driving amongst them) we attempted to catch them with a frying pan', which they found 'a bad instrument to catch fish with'. The party, remember, included a fisherman and a fishmonger; had they really gone out sailing wholly unprovided with fishing tackle? Retrospectively, one despairs. There was more to come.

Now they headed back for Jamestown. On the way down through the Bay, Smith decided to turn west up the Rappahannock River, to the village where Opechancanough had paraded him to see whether he was the tall, white captain of obnoxious memory. Unfortunately, at Smith Point, the barge was caught by the ebb tide, and grounded on a shoal. While they waited, to pass the time they tried to catch fish by spiking them with their swords, rather as they had seen the natives do, and soon 'took more in one hour than we could eat in a day'. As Smith was pulling one fish off his sword, it struck him with its tail, 'like a riding rod, wherein the midst is a most poisoned sting, of two or three inches long, bearded like a saw on each side, which she struck an inch and a half into the wrist of his arm; no blood or wound was seen but a little blue spot, but the torment was instantly so extreme, that in four hours [it] had so extremely swollen his hand, arm, shoulder and part of [his] body' that they all gave him up for dead.

Unexpectedly, an unheroic and meaningless death now confronted him. Despite the terrible agony, he remained in command, controlling the men and directing them where to dig his grave on a nearby island, 'which we called Stingray Isle, after the name of the fish'. As the others stood by helplessly, Russell applied 'a precious oil', that seemed to diminish the effects of the poison. Time passed; the light faded; the pain eased; he would live. The men lit fires of driftwood and cooked their meals, grilling or frying fresh fish caught only a few hours earlier. Smith, weak but resilient as ever, triumphed again: for his supper, he ate the stingray – 'which gave no less joy and content to us, than ease to himself'. He could have adapted Julius Caesar's boast, to 'Veni, edi, vici': I came, I ate, I conquered. Sometimes, to survive is to conquer.

When the tide rose, they pushed out into deeper water, and set off for Jamestown through the darkness, steering, as the phrase is, by guess and by God; the early morning light showed them Kecoughtan village, at the mouth of the James River. Here they were welcomed by the Indians, who saw Smith's bandaged arm and another man's bloody leg, injured in some accident, as well as the bows, arrows, shields, cloaks and furs they had acquired during their travels, and assumed that all this was the result of battle and conquest. Taking the opportunity of impressing the Indians with their military prowess, the supposed conquering heroes declared that this was what they had 'got and made of the Massawomekes', no less. Such news travelled faster than any postboy; by the time they reached Warraskoyack village, it was well known. Rising to the occasion, they then trimmed the barge with streamers and coloured cloth, so disguising its normal appearance that, next day, the watchmen at Jamestown at first, horrified sight took it for a Spanish frigate.

Arriving back on 21 July, Smith was treated by the surgeon, Anthony Bagnall – but found the colony in equally bad condition. The new colonists were all sick, from Jamestown's own poisons, and the others lame or in poor condition. People complained bitterly that President Ratcliffe's authority had 'so overswayed Mr Scrivener's discretion, as [that] our store, our time, our strength and labours was idly consumed to fulfil his fantasies', particularly in being made to build an unnecessary 'palace for his pleasure in the woods'. Hearing of the exploits of the explorers, believing that gold and the desired waterway were on the verge of discovery, impressed by Smith's leadership and determination, the cry was, that Ratcliffe should be deposed, and replaced as President by Captain Smith.

Constitutionally, this was difficult; as President, Ratcliffe had two votes, and Smith and Scrivener only one each. Exactly what happened is not clear, but in the event, Ratcliffe ceased to govern, though he still had nearly two months left to serve in office. An arrangement was set up, whereby Scrivener, who was 'ill of a calenture' (some sort of fever) would govern with the help of some 'honest officers' for the remaining two months. Despite this opportunity to organise matters as he thought best – or to preside over squabbling and bitterness – Smith was not yet ready to have this greatness thrust upon him. Hardly recovered from his injury, he insisted that he would return to his exploration, as soon as could be managed – which proved to be, in three days' time.

So, on 24 July, he set off again, with a party of 12 men, including Anas Todkill and Nathanael Powell, who later wrote an account of the expedition. As so often, the weather was against them, contrary winds forcing them to stay for two or three days with the Kecoughtans, who, believing they were on another sortie against the dreaded Massawomekes, feasted them 'with much mirth'. Always keen to impress with superior military technology, every night Smith fired off two or three rockets, with terrifying effect, so that 'the poor savages supposed nothing impossible' for this small band of warriors.

Soon they were able to move on, spending the night at Stingray Isle, before crossing the mouth of the Potomac up to the Patapsco Rover, and pushing right on to the 'heads' of the Bay. By this time, the eight newcomers were sick and incapable, leaving only five, including Smith, to handle the barge. As they crossed the Bay towards the Tockwough River, they unexpectedly encountered seven or eight canoes of aggressive-seeming Indians (who turned out to be the fearsome Massawomekes). Unable to avoid them, Smith went on the offensive, steering directly at them. Covering the deck with a tarpaulin to hide the eight sick men, he had the men's hats stuck up on sticks along the sides of the barge, to suggest a larger number, with one man stationed with two muskets between each pair of hats. The extraordinary apparition of a sailing vessel, such as they had not seen before, coming at them with only a handful of armoured white men visible, proved too much for the Massawomekes, 'staring at the sailing of our barge', who hurriedly paddled towards the shore, only to be pursued into the shallows, 'right against them'. Even then, the bearded warrior in shining armour beckoned to them, to approach.

Two braves paddled over, when each found himself unexpectedly presented with a small bell; on the report of these bellwethers, the others flocked up, all eager to trade. Soon the barge was heaped with venison, bear meat, bearskins, fish, bows and arrows, clubs and what proved to be very effective shields woven from a kind of basketwork. These canoes were not the dugouts of the southern tribes, but of birch bark cemented with gum or resin; their language was also different from the Powhatans', and almost incomprehensible. By signs they indicated that they had just returned from a raid on their enemies to the east, the Tockwoughs, showing their fresh wounds; they arranged to meet again the next day.

Having waited in vain for some time the next morning, Smith took the barge eastward, to the Tockwough River, where they soon found themselves surrounded by a fleet of canoes, the men all armed 'after their barbarous manner' against another Massawomeke assault. Despite this,

Smith called out friendly greetings in Powhatan; fortunately, one of the Tockwoughs understood, and interpreted between the two parties. Seeing the distinctive Massawomeke shields and weapons piled up, the Tockwoughs were persuaded that these were the spoils of war, and soon welcomed the Englishmen into their palisaded village, entertaining them with 'dances, songs, fruits, furs and what they had ... stretching their best abilities to express their loves'. While they were trading, Smith noticed that their hatchets and knives were made of iron and brass, unknown to the Powhatan empire; the interpreter explained that they came from the Susquehannock tribe, a 'mighty people and mortal enemies with the Massawomekes'. These people lived a couple of days' journey farther upstream of the Bay, but beyond the reach of the barge, because of rocks and shallows. Smith, of course, wanted to meet them, and asked for an interpreter who could speak Susquehannock, to interpret his interpreter, and promptly set off.

Having gone as far as they could, they waited a few days while the interpreter went on alone, to persuade some Susquehannocks to come down and trade. While waiting, they did some more exploring, until they reached a waterfall on the Susquehanna River, which he named Smith's Falls – the farthest north he reached. Within a few days, some 60 Susquehannocks and five werowances arrived, bearing gifts, including enormous ceremonial tobacco pipes, venison, baskets, shields, bows and arrows. They made a great impression, literally, seeming 'giant-like' to the English (who were generally shorter than most natives that they met). Smith wrote in the *Map of Virginia*: 'These are the most strange people of all those countries, both in language and attire; for their language, it may well beseem their proportions, sounding from them as it were a great voice in a vault or cave, as an echo. Their attire is the skins of bears and wolves ... One had the head of a wolf hanging in a chain for a jewel, his tobacco pipe three quarters of a yard long, prettily carved with a bird, a deer or some such device at the great end, sufficient to beat out the brains of a man ... The picture of the greatest of them is signified in the Map.'

They, in turn, were impressed by the great English werowance and presumed Massawomeke-killer, and agreed to accompany him back across the bay to the Tockwough village. While there, the Englishmen continued their normal practice, which was 'daily to have prayer, with a psalm; at which solemnity the poor savages much wondered'. The sight of this unfamiliar ritual of worship of an unknown but obviously extremely powerful spirit had a remarkable effect. The Susquehannas 'began in a most passionate manner to hold up their hands to the sun, with a most fearful song; then, embracing the Captain, they began to adore him in like manner. Though he rebuked them, yet they proceeded till their song was finished, which done, with a most strange, furious action and a hellish voice began an oration of their loves. That ended, with a great painted bear's skin they covered our Captain [a very short man, he would have been almost smothered in fur], then one ready with a chain of white beads (weighing at least six or seven pounds) hung it about his neck.'

Others came forward with 18 mantles of different kinds of skin sewn together, which they laid at his feet with various other gifts, 'stroking their ceremonious hands about his neck' to invest him as their governor, 'promising their aid, victuals or what they had to be his, if he would stay with them to defend and revenge them' against the Massawomekes.

Regretfully, Smith explained that he could not stay, but would try to return the next year. In the meantime, he got some information from them about other tribes living farther away, 'upon a great water beyond the mountains', which he guessed was in the direction of Canada, where they would have got their metal hatchets from the French. Now it was time to be heading back south. On the way, he acknowledged a debt to his old friends and patrons in Lincolnshire, the Berties, naming one hill 'Peregrine's Mount' and a river, 'Willoughby's River'. Down they went, quickly visiting the Patuxent River before turning westward into the Rappahannock, that the stingray had diverted him from a few weeks earlier. Thirty miles upstream, at Moraughtacund village, they met their old friend, Mosco, and took him on again as guide, interpreter and 'very present help in time of need'.

Here Mosco told Smith that he should not cross the river to the Rappahannocks, as the Moraughtacunds had recently stolen three women from them, and anyone coming from Moraughtacund would almost certainly be killed. Suspecting that Mosco was trying to keep the English trade goods for himself and his friends, Smith decided to go over, anyway.

A dozen or more Rappahannocks were waiting on the shore, who waved them to where a few beached canoes suggested a landing-place. As usual, Smith insisted upon an exchange of hostages, and four or five Indians waded out, to leave their man. The English hostage, Anas Todkill, went ashore, but went searching a little way ('two stones'-throws') inland, where he found a large number of warriors hiding behind the trees. Immediately he started to run back to the barge, but the Indians grabbed him and tried to carry him off. Todkill called out that they were betrayed, and the Indian hostage promptly jumped overboard, only to be shot dead in the water by his guard.

The Rappahannocks then started a barrage of arrows as the English fired back; Todkill threw himself on the ground as musket-balls and arrows flew over him. Smith had set up his sturdy Massawomeke shields like a forecastle on the barge, his men firing in safety from behind them. After the Indians had shot over 'a thousand' arrows in vain, they retreated into the woods, and Smith's men, still protected by Massawomeke shields, landed, picked up Todkill, unharmed but spattered with Indian blood, and pursued the Indians into the woods, finding only a few dead, and many splashes of blood.

The English then broke many of the arrows lying around, before giving most of the rest, and the abandoned canoes, to Mosco. Having realised that Massawomeke shields were practically arrow-proof, Smith now converted the barge into an armoured vessel, replacing the wooden oar-tholes with sturdy sticks like bedposts and fixing the shields to them, so concealing and protecting all on board.

Having spent the night moored offshore, the next morning they went farther upstream, with Mosco trotting along the bank before coming aboard again. Suddenly, a flight of arrows struck the boat, bouncing off the shields, as Mosco dropped flat, crying 'Rappahannocks!'. What they thought were so many bushes proved to be camouflaged Rappahannocks, who, when fired on, simply disappeared into the reeds. After half a mile, the warriors then revealed themselves, 'dancing and singing very merrily' – or triumphantly jeering.

Farther on, the English were able to do some friendly trading at other villages; sadly, one of the few gentlemen Smith had a good word for, Richard Fetherstone, died, presumably of Jamestown disease, and was buried at night, with a musket-volley salute from his healthier colleagues. Later, Smith took a reconnaissance party ashore, when suddenly, an arrow fell at the guard's feet; a prompt search showed no sign of the enemy, but the party quickly prepared themselves. In a few minutes there were a hundred 'nimble Indians skipping from tree to tree, letting fly their arrows as fast as they could'. The English fired back, while Mosco, who was with them, having shot all his arrows, made such a hullabaloo running back to the barge to get more, that the attackers thought that the English had a considerable Indian detachment with them, and made a rapid getaway through the undergrowth.

Following after them, the English found a warrior, wounded in the knee, lying 'as dead', which 'Mosco seeing, never was dog more furious against a bear [as in bear-baiting]', to beat out his brains. More mercifully, and practically, the English brought the man on board, where the surgeon, Bagnall, who had been brought along 'partly' to tend Smith's sting-ray injury, treated the wound. After Mosco had gathered up more valuable arrows, he acted as interpreter for Smith's interrogation. The man said his name was Amoroleck, of the Hassinungas, and that they had attacked because they had heard (Powhatan's influence) that the English 'were a people come from under the world, to take their world from them'. Asked how many worlds he knew, he replied that he knew no more 'but that which was under the sky that covered him, which were the Powhatans, with the Monacans and the Massawomekes, that were higher up in the mountains'. Asked what was beyond the mountains (perhaps the sea, the sea!), he answered, 'the sun; but of anything else, he knew nothing'. He then suggested the English stay on until the various local chiefs returned from a joint hunting trip, and make friends. Once again, Mosco advised against this, and was again over-ruled; he spent the evening diligently trimming his arrows.

Very soon – not to his surprise – arrows were showering down upon the barge. Smith got Mosco and Amoroleck to call out for a parley, but the yelling and hallooing were too loud for them to be heard, so the barge moved off cautiously into the night.

Daylight found them moored in a bay several miles away, out of arrow-range. After an early breakfast, they took down some Massawomeke shields and revealed themselves, armed with swords and shields, to those watching from the trees. Amoroleck called out, saying how he had been treated well and been protected from Mosco's anger, and urging friendship with these powerful visitors.

After a short while, two men swam out, presenting a bow and quiver of arrows as a sign of peace. Smith welcomed them, and suggested the other chiefs should also send such signs of friendship, which soon followed. The three chiefs received various presents; 'our pistols they took for pipes, which they much desired, but we did content them with other commodities'. Following this, Smith returned to Rappahannock territory; here, they sought friendship, but he pointed out that they had attacked him twice without provocation, and threatened that he would destroy their houses and corn unless they submitted to them, and made peace with the Moraughtacunds. He followed this by calling a general inter-tribal peace conference, with himself in charge. The different chiefs now promised peace, and the Rappahannock chief said Smith could have the three women stolen by the Moraughtacunds. Judge Solomon Smith then gave the women chains and beads, and decreed that the Rappahannock chief could keep the woman he loved best, the Moraughtacund chief could have one, and, as a bonus, Mosco could have the third, along with even more bows and arrows. A party was agreed for the next day – 'away went their canoes over the water, to fetch their venison and all the provision they could' – when a good time was had by all, especially Mosco, who celebrated by changing his name to Uttasantasough, meaning, 'Stranger – for so they call us'.

It was time to go back; crossing the Bay at night, they were caught in a sudden, extreme gust of thunder and rain, and once again had to bale out water frantically, 'never thinking to escape drowning'. As on the way out, they called in at Kecoughtan for rest and feeding, before Smith decided to go visiting more neighbours near home. First, he sailed south-east to the creeks and forests of the Chesapeake homeland, but, finding no-one in, turned westward to the Nansemond River. Here, they saw half a dozen men working on their fish-traps, who fled at the sight of them, before returning to pick up the 'divers toys' that were put out for them. One came on board, and invited Smith to visit his home upriver, the others following on shore 'with all show of love that could be'. After seven or eight miles they reached a little island, where they were greeted by the man's wife and children; other Indians now invited them to their houses, farther up, where the river narrowed. Smith tried to get some to come on board, as a safety precaution; eventually they said they had to go ashore to fetch their bows and arrows, but then would not come back aboard. His suspicions of a trap were justified: seven or eight canoes full of armed men appeared behind them, and arrows flew 'so fast as two or three hundred could shoot them'. Smith managed to turn round, and went for them, firing with great speed and so effectively that many jumped overboard, while others paddled away as fast as they could. At this point, the river passed through flat, open land, with no cover for the Indians, who went into hiding behind some trees, leaving the English in possession of the island.

They now captured the Nansemonds' canoes, and moored them nearby, before discussing tactics. They might be facing a large force: should they set fire to the island immediately, or enforce a truce and payment of corn? Choosing the latter, they began to chop up the hard-made, dugout canoes, which brought about an immediate response. Smith now demanded the wereowance's bow and arrows, as tokens of submission, a chain of pearls, and a promise of 400 baskets of corn on his next visit, coupled with a threat to destroy all their canoes, houses and corn. The Indian negotiators agreed, but said they had to have a canoe to bring what he had demanded, so he pushed one adrift, and told them to swim for it; in the meantime, the chopping would continue. Appalled, the Indians immediately submitted, giving up their bows and arrows, while 'tag and rag' came with baskets of corn. Having taken all they could carry, the English left, 'departing good friends', as Smith wrote – and, no doubt, leaving behind more bitter enemies.

That evening, 7 September, they sailed into Jamestown moorings. Here they found that Ratcliffe had been arrested for 'mutiny', presumably an attempt to regain control. Scrivener had seen to it that the harvest, such as it was, had been gathered, but much of the stores and provisions had been spoiled by rain getting into the poorly maintained storehouse. Smith's expedition had been useful in developing knowledge of the area, and establishing relationships with some of the tribes. His absence had not directly helped matters in Jamestown, but demonstrated the need for good order and authority, that it appeared only he could supply. September 10th would be election day, when he would become President Smith.

11

Love You Not Me?

In the words of Chapter VII of *The Proceedings of the English Colonie in Virginia*, 'The 10 of September, 1608, by the election of the Council, and request of the company, Captain Smith received the letters patent, and took upon him the place of President; which till then by no means he would accept, though he was often importuned thereunto.'

The new broom began with some vigorous sweeping: the Ratcliffe 'palace', whatever it was, was immediately discontinued, the church and leaky storehouse repaired, new storehouses built for the expected supplies from England, the fortifications reconstructed, and the 'order of watch' reorganised. Men were now also exercised every Saturday in military techniques 'on the plain by the west bulwark we called Smithfield', to the amazement of the watching Indians, as Smith supervised musket practice, 'battering' luckless target trees. The boats were better equipped for trading purposes, and, at the end of the month, George Percy, now with the title of Lieutenant, was sent off in one down the James River – where, to his surprise, he encountered Newport, breezing across the Bay in the *Mary and Margaret* with 70 new colonists.

Newport was not expected back so soon, but the Council in London had been keen to get him there as soon as possible. Early in July, Captain Nelson had brought Smith's first sketch-map of the area, together with his letter, that, after some confusion, got published on 13 August as the

True Relation; Newport had reported that Powhatan had suggested to Smith that there was a route to the South Sea through Chesapeake Bay; and John Martin had reported excitedly, if over-optimistically, of the possibilities of gold. The Council was impatient for results. So here was Newport, with new, firm instructions from the Council, addressed to 'The President'.

Smith was not happy – to say the least – with this letter and what Newport had to say; when Newport eventually returned to England, he carried what even Smith called a 'rude' letter of reply. From that, the contents of the Council's letter can be reconstructed. The Council reproved the colonists for dissension and 'factions'; the President was to obey Newport's instructions; two new councillors had been sent out, Captain Richard Waldo and Captain Peter Winne, described by Smith as 'ancient [experienced] soldiers and valiant gentlemen, but ignorant of the business'. In particular, as Smith later phrased it, Newport had been told 'not to return without a lump of gold, a certainty of the South Sea or one of the lost company of Sir Walter Ralegh' – perhaps to be discovered with the aid of a hefty new, collapsible barge, intended to be carried in five sections past waterfalls and shallows and then reconstructed for sailing up inland rivers and possible seas. To crown it all, there were elaborate presents for Powhatan: a bedstead and mattress, a washbasin and ewer, and other costly 'novelties' – and an actual crown. The Council in London thought it would be a good idea to crown Powhatan as a king, intending to arouse his gratitude and, though he would not realise it, make him a subordinate to his new overlord, King James (the thinking was much the same as when Powhatan made Smith a werowance in his tribe). Smith knew his man better than that: the way to gain Indians' respect was not through trying to ingratiate oneself, but by demonstrating equal strength; as it was, 'this stately kind of soliciting made him so much overvalue himself, that he respected us as much as nothing at all'.

Smith certainly made his views known, but had to submit to the new régime. Newport had Ratcliffe reinstated to the council, so that, with the new councillors, Smith could be out-voted, and more time spent in preparations for the forthcoming coronation. The London Council had demanded that the ship return with commodities to the value of £2,000, to defray expenses: the colony was to produce quantities of clapboard, soap-ashes, pitch, tar and glass; Smith enquired when all this was to be done. Furthermore, the 70 new colonists (including foreign workmen, and an English lady and her maid) would need feeding, and more provisions had to be obtained. Newport, now definitely no friend of Smith, suggested that Smith merely wanted to reserve for himself any credit for obtaining supplies, and was being obstructive, whilst 'the cruelty he had used to the savages might well be the occasion to hinder these designs, and seek revenge on him'. As for provisions, on Newport's return from Werocomoco, he would load the pinnace with corn, and even add supplies from his ship. So there.

In an attempt to demonstrate helpfulness, and perhaps make Powhatan more amenable, Smith now volunteered to go first to Werocomoco, together with Waldo, two other gentlemen and a lad, together with Namontack, now returned from his visit to England, to persuade Powhatan to come to Jamestown for his coronation. When they got there, they were told that Powhatan and his men were away hunting, so Smith asked for a messenger to be sent. While the Englishmen were waiting, the young women of the village offered to entertain them.

As the five sat before a fire in a field, there was 'a hideous noise and shrieking' from the surrounding woods, that made them grab their weapons, fearing a surprise attack, but little Pocahontas came to reassure them that no harm was intended. Then 30 young women came running out, naked but for a few green leaves strategically placed before and behind, their bodies all painted in red, white, black or piebald. In a parody of male hunters and dancers, they all had stags' antlers on their heads; one had an otter skin at her waist and arm, with a quiver of arrows and a bow; others had swords and clubs, one, even, a pot-stick (for stirring). With 'hellish cries and shouts' they danced and sang round the fire, with 'most excellent ill variety', for nearly an hour, before withdrawing into the woods again. Having dressed again, they returned and 'invited

Smith to their lodging' (he does not say whether his colleagues were also invited), where, he wrote, 'all these nymphs more tormented him than ever, with crowding and pressing, and hanging upon him, most tediously crying, Love you not me? Love you not me?' Most men in their late twenties could think of worse torments than this, even if these bold, underdressed young women were only teasing. After this, there was a large feast of meat, fish, fruit and beans, before they conducted him with 'firebrands' to his lodging. It is worth remarking that, as several commentators observed, it was common practice for Indian women to sleep with honoured visitors; some, at least, of these visitors may have enjoyed this custom. (It is not the sort of thing that Smith, reported as noticeably priggish about drinking and swearing, would mention.)

The next day, Powhatan returned; old chief and new president greeted each other in appropriate fashion, before Smith returned Namontack to him, told him about the presents that Newport had brought, invited him to come to Jamestown and also to join forces in Newport's proposed attack upon the old enemy, the Monacans. Powhatan was very much upon his dignity: he was a king, and Newport was to come to him to give the presents; he could deal with the Monacans by himself, when he wished; and as for 'any salt water beyond the mountains, the relations you have had from my people are false'. After some polite chit-chat, Smith returned to Jamestown.

Newport now had the presents, too bulky to carry overland, packed and sent round by water, a journey of over 80 miles, but came himself the shorter route through the woods, with a guard of 50 men, to await their arrival. At last, everything was ready for the coronation. The wash-basin and ewer, the great bed and mattress were set up, and a scarlet cloak produced (it took Namontack, the sophisticated traveller, to reassure Powhatan that it would not harm him to put it on). Presumably some ritual words were intoned, but when it came to the actual crowning, Powhatan refused to kneel, or even bend the knee, to receive the crown. The English tried 'persuasions, examples and instructions', but to no avail. At last someone had the nerve to lean hard upon his shoulders, so that he stooped a little, and the crown was popped on. For the finishing touch to this farce, someone fired a pistol as a signal for a musket salute from the barge, causing Powhatan to start 'in a horrible fear'. Calm and smiles were restored, and King Powhatan reciprocated Newport's gifts with his mantle and a pair of his old shoes (*noblesse oblige*).

On a more practical level, Newport once again asked for assistance in his expedition into Monacan territory, but was only granted Namontack as a guide and seven or eight baskets of corn (while the English bought another half-dozen). Smith is unlikely to have been surprised by this limited response. Once back in Jamestown, Newport selected the 120 fittest men, with Waldo, Percy, Winne, Scrivener and young Francis West (younger brother of Lord De La Warr, himself soon to become important in Jamestown affairs), and set off, leaving behind the colony's most experienced explorer and Indian fighter, with some 80 less fit men, 'such as they were', to reload the ship with clapboard. The expedition got as far as the waterfalls, where the 120 prepared to portage their five-piece barge. As Smith wrote sardonically in his letter, 'If he had burned her to ashes, one might have carried her in a bag; but as she is, five hundred cannot, to a navigable place above the falls.' They left the barge, and tramped on into the Monacan woodlands; here they had no great success, in fact being reduced to employing methods more alienating than Smith's, when they seized a chief, bound him and forced him to act as a guide. There was no way through to the sea; there was no gold or silver. They had a refiner with them, who thought he had found a little silver, and that 'better stuff might be had for the digging'. Newport had to settle for that; having marched his men up the hill, he marched them down again. Returning past the falls and their heap of lumber, he found not only no corn awaiting him, but no Indians willing to trade at any price. So much for his confident boasts. Back they all came, 'half sick, all complaining and tired with toil, famine and discontent, to have only but discovered our gilded hopes and such fruitless certainties as Captain Smith foretold us'.

President Smith promptly sent the fittest of them to get on with the new industrial work, preparing to make glass, tar, pitch and soap-ashes, and then went off himself with 30 others, five miles downriver, to live in the woods and chop trees for clapboard. The work-party included several newly-arrived gentlemen, wholly inexperienced in physical labour, some of whom however, following the example of former yeoman Smith, did quite well. Two of them, Gabriel Beadell and John Russell, 'the only two gallants of this last supply' ('gallant' was not a complimentary term in Smith's vocabulary) even gained his praise, as they took to the work, 'making it their delight to hear the trees thunder as they fell' (it was important to present the gentlemen as only amusing themselves). Unfortunately, handling the axes blistered their soft hands, so that 'commonly every third blow had a loud oath to drown the echo'. Prim Smith set up a swear-bath, whereby for each oath a can of water was poured down the offender's sleeve, so that soon the party was clean in mouth and limb. He wrote that 30 or so gentleman volunteers, working not as labourers but ostensibly 'only as a pleasure and recreation' were more use than 100 pressed men – 'but twenty good workmen had been better than all'.

When he got back to Jamestown, it was to find that no-one had thought to do anything much about renewing the provisions ('the ship lay idle and would do nothing'), so immediately he took a barge up the Chickahominy, to trade, with instructions for Percy to follow. However, in accordance with Powhatan's policy of starving out the English, 'that dogged nation' refused to trade. Refusing to be thwarted, Smith told them that he had not come to trade but to punish them for their attack on him and his men the previous winter, and landed his 18 men for the assault. The Chickahominies fled, but soon returned with 100 bushels of corn, fish and fowl, before also filling Percy's barge, when that arrived.

Having delivered these supplies, he then learned that some people (he suggests Newport and Ratcliffe) resented his success in trading, and suggested that because he had left the fort – to chop wood and trade for food – without the permission of the council, he should be deposed and banished; this malicious absurdity was soon quashed: 'their horns were too short'. Apart from this, another major problem had become all too apparent. Colonists had been trading with the ship's sailors, bartering furs, baskets and squirrels for butter, cheese, meat, beer, aquavitae and biscuits. The furs should have gone into the storehouse as part of the goods to be paid to the London Council, but were sold privately; one ship's master later sold his furs for £30, more than he had been paid for the entire voyage. The corruption began at the top: 'and had not Captain Newport cried *Peccavi* [admitted fault], the President would have discharged the ship and caused him to have stayed one year in Virginia, to learn to speak of his own experience' (so wrote Smith later, though it is doubtful that he could have enforced this). Perhaps even worse, some colonists had bought their trade furs from the Indians with metal tools – hatchets, chisels, pickaxes – as well as, even more dangerously, pikeheads, knives, shot and gunpowder.

It was more than time for Newport to be gone. Scrivener went with Namontack to Werocomoco to buy some corn, only to find the residents more inclined to fight than to trade, and came away with only three or four hogsheads. As it was, the colonists had to give the ship three hogsheads of corn for the return journey.

At last, some time in December, Newport left, taking with him his friend Ratcliffe ('lest the company should cut his throat', wrote Smith), clapboard and other materials intended to defray costs, Smith's excellent 'Map of Chesapeake Bay and Rivers' and, no doubt, carefully sealed, Smith's vigorous letter of reply to the Council. In this, he begins by responding to the criticism of factions: 'unless you would have me run away and leave the country, I cannot prevent them, because I do make many stay that would else fly any whither'. He has sent back troublemaker Ratcliffe – 'what he is, now everyone can tell you'; 'if he and Archer return again, they are sufficient to keep us always in factions'.

Much of the letter is taken up with attacking Newport, whose latest voyage has cost the company £2,000, which cannot be compensated by the clapboard, pitch, tar and soap-ashes Smith has sent (incidentally pointing out that the colony cannot compete commercially with Russia and Sweden, the main sources of timber). Newport had failed to find a

South Sea route, gold or the lost colonists; his grand expedition of 120 men achieved no more than might have been done by one man, 'for the value of a pound of copper'. Smith claims to have made 'as great discovery [the Chesapeake Bay map] as he, for less charge than he spendeth every meal'. Against his better judgement, Smith had obeyed instructions to do what Newport wanted, 'I fear to the hazard of us all'; the clumsy coronation of Powhatan would only cause trouble. Newport had promised to load the barges with corn, but came back with only 14 bushels; his ship's crew had kept and sold on supplies intended for the colonists, so in future the company should let the colonists know what they were due to receive, so that they should not 'stand to the sailors' courtesy to leave us what they please'. Furthermore, considering that any ship's master 'can find the way as well as he', the company would save money by no longer employing expensive Captain Newport.

The colonists had a poor diet and limited resources: for all the birds, fish and game in the area, 'we [present writer excluded, of course] are so weak and ignorant, we cannot much trouble them'. The next supply of colonists needed to be working men – carpenters, husbandmen, fishermen, blacksmiths, diggers – rather than gallants and gentlemen, 'such as we have', who used up resources 'before they can be made good for anything'. He concludes with a blunt warning: 'as yet you must not look for any profitable returns: so I humbly rest.'

Humility and modesty were never remarkable among Smith's characteristics; the lords, knights and gentlemen recipients of his letter were likely to find it somewhat too 'rude' in tone for their taste, especially with its implicit criticisms of gentlemen, and their own policies. Nevertheless, his report could generally be believed, and his capabilities were apparent; but, clearly there were serious problems at Jamestown. There would have to be changes.

12

There Comes Captain Smith

In the meantime, in mid-December, President Smith had to consider the welfare of the 200 colonists who were his responsibility, in particular the constant need for provisions to get them through the winter. The Nansemonds were only 30 miles downriver; when Smith, with Scrivener and Captain Winne, went to trade, they refused, despite earlier promises: the harvest had been poor, they had none to spare and, more ominously, Powhatan had ordered them not to. Impatiently, Smith ordered his men to fire a musket-volley, when the villagers ran off into the woods; he then went ashore and burned a hut, which brought them back again, to buy him off. Eventually, they managed to load three boats with 100 bushels of corn – better than nothing, but nowhere near enough. The relentless quest for food went on, whatever the conditions:

'So we returned to our quarter some four miles down the river, which was only the open woods under the lee of a hill, where all the ground was covered with snow, and hard frozen. The snow we digged away and made a great fire in the place; when the ground was well dried, we turned away the fire, and, covering the place with a mat, there we lay very warm. To keep us from the wind we made a shade of another mat; as the wind turned, we turned our shade, and when the ground grew cold we [re] moved the fire. And thus many a cold winter night have we lain in this miserable manner, yet those that most commonly went upon all these occasions were always in health, lusty and fat.' (The more time spent away from Jamestown's miasma and poisons, the better for one's health.)

Returning to unload, and having attended the first Christian marriage in America, between John Laydon, one of the original settlers, and Anne Burras (Burrowes, Burroughs), the lady's maid, Smith fitted out two barges for himself and Captain Waldo to go trading up the James River. There they found that the Weanocs, 'that churlish nation', had gone into hiding to avoid them; the Appomattocs sold them a little. Another expedition by Scrivener and Percy had no success at all. Clearly, Powhatan's starvation policy was behind this. Smith decided to 'surprise', that is, to raid, Powhatan, with Waldo ('sure in time of need'), only to find that Scrivener and Winne were against this, either in accordance with the London Council's policy or, as Smith suspected, in Scrivener's case, jealous ambition (in an idiom derived from Cesare Borgia's motto, seeking 'to make himself either Caesar or nothing'). At this point, Powhatan himself intervened. Guessing that the colonists would by now be in considerable difficulties, he sent a message that he was prepared to load the English ship with corn, in return for some men to build him a new, European-style house at Werocomoco, with a grindstone, 50 swords, some 'pieces' (muskets), a cock and hen, some copper and beads. In the circumstances, he reckoned it was an offer Smith could not refuse; yet, whatever the circumstances, Smith could not accept it in its entirety.

Powhatan seemed to have them over the proverbial (if, in this case, empty) barrel. Although 'not ignorant of his devices and subtlety', Smith now sent a party of men, including three of the new foreign ('Dutch', as they called them) arrivals, to start work on the house. Leaving Scrivener in charge of those sulking in Jamestown, Smith followed on himself with 46 volunteers ('they all knowing Smith would not return empty', as he boasted), himself in the *Discovery* barge with six gentlemen and six soldiers, with Percy, West and William Fettiplace in the pinnace, and a dozen more in the other barge. It was 29 December, in the deep mid-winter: frosty wind made moan, earth stood hard as iron, water like a stone (snow had fallen, etc: this was in the very middle of what climatologists call the Little Ice Age).

They spent the first night at Warraskoyack village, where the werowance was friendly, and even warned Smith against his mission: 'You shall find Powhatan to use you kindly, but trust him not, and be sure he hath no opportunity to seize on your arms, for he hath sent for you only to cut your throats.' The advice was unnecessary, but suggested goodwill; Smith then asked for guides to escort one Master Michael Sicklemore (apparently no relation to John Sicklemore/Ratcliffe) to the werowance of Chawanoac, south of the river, hoping still for news of Roanoke survivors. He also left his page, Samuel Collier, to learn the language.

The next day they sailed on, only to encounter such severe weather – gales, sleet, ice and snow – that they sheltered at Kecoughtan for six or seven days, until Twelfth Night, where they apparently had a good time. 'We were never more merry, nor fed on more plenty of good oysters, fish, flesh, wildfowl and good bread, nor never had better fires in England than in the dry, warm, smoky houses' of Kecoughtan. Smith noted that, while there, he, Surgeon Bagnall and Sergeant Pising shot 148 wildfowl; one hopes that a good proportion went to the Kecoughtans in recompense for their unforeseen hospitality. Hardly had they got away when the terrible winter gales returned, driving them to impose themselves on the Kiskiacks, despite their new hosts' unwillingness. On 12 January they reached Werocomoco, to find the river frozen half a mile from the shore. Undeterred, Smith forced his way through the ice, until the ebb tide left his barge stranded on the 'oozy shoals'. Rather than stay there 'frozen to death', he then made his men follow him in wading waist deep through the icy mud to the shore. John Russell, already unwell and overweight, was exhausted and chilled to numbness, but recovered in the warmth of the nearest houses, where Powhatan had them sent food. When the tide rose again, Smith had the barge hoisted on board the pinnace.

The next day, Powhatan received them, politely offering food as usual, but asking when they would be on their way: he had not sent for them, and had no corn – but for 40 swords he could manage 40 baskets of corn. In the face of this cheek, Smith pointed out amongst Powhatan's entourage the men who had brought his message, and asked how he could be so forgetful. The chief brushed this off with 'a merry laugh' (it must have been like joking with Stalin), before turning to trading. Exploiting his advantage, he set stiff terms, demanding guns and swords, saying he could eat his corn but not Smith's copper. Smith's response was to say that, out of goodwill, he had sent men to build Powhatan's new house, although Powhatan appeared to want to starve him out. He could not spare any swords or guns, as he needed them for himself, but would not break friendship, unless forced. Powhatan then said how he had been told that Smith's coming was not for trade, but 'to invade my people and possess my country'. His people were afraid of Smith's guns, but if Smith would leave his weapons on board, they would 'all be friends and for ever Powhatans' (a reminder that Smith was supposed to be one of his werowances). And so the day passed away in futile manoeuvring.

The next morning, Smith went to inspect work on Powhatan's new house, and found that surprisingly little progress had been made, even taking into account the recent bad weather. What was going on was not clear then, but became more apparent some time later. The supply ship had brought several foreign workmen, some described as 'Dutch', a term applied by the English to Hollanders, Germans and Swiss indiscriminately. One of these was considered by Smith to be of such 'spirit, judgement and resolution' that he 'knew not whom better to trust', and accordingly sent him with the work-party as a spy. However, while at Werocomoco, the 'Dutchmen' had decided that, the food situation being what it was, the English could not survive without Powhatan, whilst he could destroy the English, and that they would do better by transferring allegiance to him, letting him know the Englishmen's situation and intentions. Presumably they thought – if 'thought' is not too strong a word – that after the English were all dead or gone, he would keep alive such cowardly traitors. In the meantime, building work was accordingly slowed down, as they stayed quietly at Werocomoco, waiting for Powhatan and/or the winter to finish off the English.

This was not yet known to Smith, when he began the day's bargaining, during which he managed to 'wrangle out of the king ten quarters of corn for a copper kettle'. There then ensued a lengthy debate, later written up in some style – but the gist of the speeches seems probable and convincing. Powhatan began with a lengthy, thoughtful speech of persuasion, how having seen 'the death of all my people thrice [presumably in three earlier wars], and not one living of those three generations but myself, I know the difference of peace and war better than any in my country'. If Smith attempted to take what he wanted by force, they could hide in the forests, and the colonists would starve; but obviously it would be better for him, he said, 'to eat good meat, lie well and sleep quietly with my women and children, laugh and be merry with you, have copper, hatchets or what I want, being your friend, than be forced to fly from all, to lie cold in the woods, feed upon acorn, roots and such trash, and be so hunted by you, that I can neither rest, eat nor sleep, but my tired men must watch, and if a twig but break, everyone crieth, there cometh Captain Smith.' So, let us be friends, and put away your guns and swords.

Unmoved, Smith responded that, unlike himself, Powhatan had broken his promises, but that, for his sake, Smith had prevented any vengeful punishment – and Powhatan would know 'as well the cruelty we use to our enemies, as our true love to our friends'. Powhatan's men came to Jamestown carrying their weapons without the English taking exception to what was their own custom. If it came to war, that for the English was their 'chiefest pleasure', and, as for the Powhatans trying to hide their provisions in the woods, the Englishmen had 'a rule to find', beyond their knowledge.

So the haggling began again, but, seeing that the guns and guards remained, Powhatan tried yet again, and 'sighing, breathed his mind once more' (so Sisyphus must have sighed, before pushing his boulder uphill yet again). He had never treated any of his werowances as well as Smith, yet received the least kindness from him. Even Captain Newport had given him swords and copper, and sent away his guns when asked, but not Smith, who insisted on having his own way. He went on, 'Captain Newport you call father, and so you call me, but I see for all us both, you will do what you list, and we must seek to content you.' He concluded with an emotive plea to put away the guns, designed to pluck the heartstrings: 'You see the love I bear you doth cause me thus nakedly forget myself.'

Despite this, and having no cause to trust him, Smith was certain that Powhatan was merely manoeuvring 'to cut his throat'. Accordingly, he got the Indians to break the ice, so that the boats could fetch him and the corn he had bought, and instructed more of his men to come ashore to him, to confront Powhatan. His reply, as recorded, was firm, implicitly denying any claim on him as an Indian werowance. 'Powhatan, you must know, as I have but one God, I honour but one king; and I live not here as your subject but as your friend, to pleasure you with what I can.' When he came to visit, the next day, he would leave behind his arms, as a sign of trust in his 'father', but 'the small care you had of such a child caused my men persuade me to look to myself'.

Powhatan now withdrew, leaving two or three women to chat to Smith, while some warriors now quietly surrounded the longhouse, to ambush Smith when he emerged. On discovering this, Smith's response was characteristically vigorous, as 'with his pistol, sword and target he made such a passage among these naked devils that they fled before him, some one way, some another, so that without hurt' he reached his bodyguard (only 18 men). The Indians now came up and made excuses for the misunderstanding; an old man brought a large bracelet and pearl necklaces from Powhatan, and an 'ancient orator' made a speech, explaining that Powhatan had run away in fear of Smith's guns and men, but sent his warriors to guard Smith's corn from being stolen (a likely story). Although some Powhatans had been hurt as a result of Smith's mistake, they could still be friends, if only he would take away his guns. Several braves, 'goodly well-proportioned fellows, as grim as devils', followed up by offering to guard the corn against any (improbable) theft, but the sight of the Englishmen cocking their muskets made them drop their bows and arrows, and hurriedly carry the corn on board. Once again, the boat was caught by the ebb tide and stuck on the mud, so that the English would have to wait until the midnight tide would float them off. The Indians offered them a longhouse to rest in, and to feast and entertain them.

For all the smiles, Powhatan was preparing 'to surprise the house and him at supper. Notwithstanding, the eternal all-seeing God did prevent him, and by a strange means. For Pocahontas, his dearest jewel and daughter, in that dark night came through the irksome woods, and told our captain great cheer should be sent us by and by, but Powhatan and all the power he could make would after come and kill us all, if they that brought it could not kill us with our own weapons when we were at supper.' Smith rather thoughtlessly offered her the kind of presents he knew she liked, but 'with tears running down her cheeks, she said she durst not be seen to have any: for if Powhatan should know it, she were but dead', and slipped away by herself, back into the darkness. An adolescent crush on Smith seems an inadequate explanation for her transfer of loyalty from family and tribe to the alien Englishmen.

Soon enough, eight or ten men arrived with platters of venison and other food, keen that the Englishmen should put out the smoking matches for their muskets, as they disliked the smoke, and enjoy their meal. Instead, Smith made them taste every dish that they had brought, and sent some of them back to Powhatan to tell him that he knew of his plans, and was ready for him. At high tide, they were able to get away, everyone still absurdly pretending to be friends. In fact, they not only left the 'Dutchmen' there to get on with the house, but also poor Edward Brinton with his musket, to shoot wildfowl for Powhatan, promising to return after they had tried their luck up the Pamunkey – ice and snow permitting.

No sooner had they gone than Powhatan sent two of the 'Dutchmen', named Adam and Franz, to Jamestown, with instructions to tell Captain Winne that all was well, but that Captain Smith had commandeered their arms, and they needed replacements, as well as more tools and clothing. These were given them, and while they were there they got talking to some six or seven likely prospects willing to sacrifice the colony for their own survival. These men then stole some swords, pike-heads, guns, shot and powder, and passed them to Indians hiding outside the fort, waiting to carry them away. The Dutchmen then returned to Werocomoco, where Powhatan had a large stock of tomahawks and swords, as well as eight pikes and eight muskets. The two Englishmen at the camp, Richard Savage and Edward Brinton, realised what was happening, and tried to get to Jamestown with a warning, but were quickly captured in the woods; rather surprisingly, they were not put to death.

Meanwhile, Smith and his men had arrived at Pamunkey, where they were entertained for two or three days by Opechancanough. It was arranged that the Englishmen, leaving the barges and pinnace in the charge of Master William Fettiplace, would meet the chief to trade at his house, a quarter of a mile inland from the river, but when they got there, they found no-one except a lame man and a boy. Then Opechancanough, who had had plenty of time to learn of developments at Werocomoco, arrived with a crowd of armed warriors. Smith began 'negotiations' promptly, telling Opechancanough that he had broken his promise to supply him with corn, and indicating his own determination: 'You know my want, and I your plenty, of which by some means I must have part; remember it is fit for kings to keep their promises.' At first trading went reasonably well, with Opechancanough promising more corn to be delivered the next day; the next morning, Smith went to the house, with 15 men as guards, where they found four or five men with large, well-loaded baskets. The chief kept them talking with 'a strained cheerfulness', until John Russell hurried in, aghast, to tell them that they were betrayed, and some 600–700 armed warriors were surrounding the house. Opechancanough's fearful expression revealed that he had guessed what Russell had said.

Smith's companions were understandably very alarmed, but he sought to rally them with a stirring speech. He began, he wrote, by complaining of the 'malicious council with their open-mouthed friends' back in England, who would accuse him of being a peace-breaker if he were to fight back. He then pointed out that if they attacked immediately, taking the chief, and each of them killing a man, and more, all the rest would run away: they would be left with so many dead bodies, and no corn for the colony. They need not be afraid of the Indians' fury: when he had been captured alone, he had outfaced 200–300 and made them come to terms; but 'we now are 16 and they but 700 at the most', so the odds had decidedly improved. If they kept their nerve and merely fired their muskets, the smoke would be enough to frighten off the Indians. If the worst came to the worst, they should fight like men, and not die like sheep, 'for by that means you know God hath oft delivered me, and so I trust will now'. Whatever this did for his men's spirits, the defenders at Rorke's Drift would have approved.

He then turned to Opechancanough, telling him that he knew the chief wanted to kill him, but, fortunately, no-one had been hurt, as yet. He then issued a challenge, that would improve the odds even more: the two of them would put aside their shields – 'my body shall be as naked as yours' – and they would fight it out, hand to hand, on a little island on the nearby river, 'and the conqueror of us two shall be lord and master of all our men'. The stakes would be Opechancanough's corn against Smith's trade copper: winner to take all.

With his large force outside the longhouse and bodyguard of some 50 men inside, Opechancanough was hardly likely to risk himself in single combat, and 'be staged to the show against a sworder', any more than Octavius Caesar against Mark Antony. There is no knowing whether Smith, banking on his Turkish exploits, seriously thought that the chief might take the gamble, or was simply attempting to gain psychological superiority. In any case, Opechancanough avoided the challenge, and pretended to appease him by offering a great present, which, he said, was just outside the door, ready for him to collect (to say nothing of 30 men, 'each his arrow nocked, ready to shoot'). A soldier, told to look outside, was too scared to go, so, leaving Percy, West and others on guard inside, Smith 'in such a rage' suddenly seized the chief by his long lock of hair, thrust his cocked pistol against his breast, and pushed him, 'near dead with fear', out before his horrified people. Opechancanough dropped his own bow and submitted, as did all his warriors at his command.

Smith then subjected them to one of his harangues, designed to intimidate, to this effect (allowances made for the limitations of his knowledge of Powhatan, and any later polishing): 'I see, you Pamunkeys, the great desire you have to kill me', which his patience had made them bold enough to try. He had promised to be their friend, until given just cause to become their enemy. 'If I keep this vow, my God will keep me, you cannot hurt me; if I break it, he will destroy me. But if you shoot one arrow to shed one drop of blood of any of my men ... you shall see I will not cease revenge, if once I begin, so long as I can ... find one of your nation ... . If I be the mark you aim at, here I stand, shoot he that dare.' They had promised to load his boat with corn, 'and so you shall, or I mean to load her with your dead carcasses.' If they traded in friendship, he would not hurt them.

Once again, sheer force of personality and will had overturned overwhelming odds, as the villagers hurried to trade, keeping him busy for two or three hours. Exhausted by nervous strain, he retired to rest in the longhouse; taking their chance, some 40 armed braves crept into the house. The noise woke him; with sword and shield and the help of a couple of comrades, he drove them out. It is perhaps worth remarking that there were plenty of Englishmen on this trip, not all of them friends of his, of whom none ever said, then or later, that these exploits did not happen.

The rest of the day passed quietly, as the Pamunkeys brought in their baskets of provisions, and Opechancanough went through the motions of polite entertainment. Then, as darkness fell, an unexpected visitor, Richard Wiffin, arrived with confidential news for the President. Nine days after Smith had left Jamestown, Scrivener had gone across the river in a boat, to the Isle of Hogs (where the colonists kept their herd of pigs), with Captain Waldo, Anthony Gosnold (Bartholomew's brother) and eight others, leaving Winne in charge. A violent storm suddenly blew up, the waves swamping the overloaded boat, which sank, taking all aboard with it. Some Indians came to the fort the next day, to report finding the boat and the bodies. At first, no-one was willing to risk the journey through the snow-choked forest and Indian territory, to report to the President; eventually, Richard Wiffin volunteered. The journey was extremely difficult and dangerous – he had to stay one night at Weroco-moco, where he was hidden by Pocahontas, who even misdirected those searching for him; there he realised the danger that they were all in. After three more days' travel, helped by Pocahontas's 'means and extraordi-nary bribes', he reached Smith at Pamunkey, and made his report; Smith ordered him not to tell anyone else.

At dawn the next day, the fields around the village were covered with people with baskets of produce, inviting the Englishmen to come ashore to trade – but only if Smith came ashore, and the Englishmen were unarmed. Needing the produce, Smith arranged that the pinnace and barge were set up with 'ambuscadoes' (shields concealing armed men), and went ashore unarmed, with Percy, West and Russell a little way behind, not obviously armed; other men went ashore to collect the goods. The crowds now gathered round him eagerly, but he unobtrusively moved back, closer to the bank and his 'ambuscadoes'. The werowance then sent a message, inviting him to come and join him, which he would not do, so the Indian had to come forward himself. This movement was not as friendly as it might have seemed, as he was accompanied by a large force of warriors in two half-moons, forming a pincer movement, with, in front, a score of men and women carrying great baskets. When this little party got close, they dropped their baskets and ran, clearing the way, as the warriors now clearly appeared. In their turn, they now saw Smith, with his three supporters aiming their guns at them, and the ambuscado soldiers behind. Never very confident when facing Smith and guns, the Indians fled.

The last basketfuls were brought on board, and Smith then told the others the news from Jamestown, ordering three gentlemen to take the barge down to Jamestown with supplies and messages of reassurance (on the way, they ran into some men sneaking off to join Powhatan, who then thought it better to return with them). Hearing the barge set off in the night, the Pamunkeys thought that Smith had sent for reinforcements to destroy them. In the morning, a messenger arrived with a chain of pearls for Smith, and promises to load the pinnace with yet more food. Over the next few days, parties came in from near and far, despite the extreme cold and deep snow, carrying the promised loads 'on their naked backs'. That was one tactic; but Opechancanough and the local werowance had another string to their bow: poison. There was a ceremonial farewell feast, after which, Smith, West and several others were stricken with sickness. All, however, recovered. One young Indian, the chief's son, swaggered insultingly with his friends, but Smith caught him and 'did not only beat, but spurned him like a dog, as scorning to do him any more mischief'. The youth ran off, while other villagers apologetically brought in more foodstuffs. Once again, a confident manner had carried the day, in a conflict where bluff and a steady nerve counted for more than main force.

Smith then decided to 'surprise' Powhatan at Werocomoco, and get some more provisions out of him, sending Wiffin and Thomas Coe ahead to spy out the land. However, Powhatan had made a strategic withdrawal, abandoning his new house and the village, carrying off all his food supplies and leaving behind only empty storehouses and a few hostile villagers. There was nothing for it but to send a messenger on ahead, overland, to warn of his imminent return, and then sail round the headland and back to Jamestown.

Smith – or his supporters – later provided a sort of balance-sheet for the expedition. For the expenditure of some 25 pounds of copper and 50 pounds of iron and beads, they wrote, they had kept some 40 men for six weeks (29 December to 9 February) on bread, corn, meat, fish and fowl, and brought back two hundredweight of deer suet and 479 bushels of corn. Recognising the rapacity of some stay-at-home adventurers and investors, Smith remarked sarcastically that 'some may think we were too charitable in not slaughtering the Indians, and disappointing in not finding heaps of gold and silver', but pointed out that the Spanish had been able to pillage a developed civilisation already rich in gold and silver, whilst their task had been one of discovery, of subduing the native hunter-agrarian natives and establishing a colony. Smith concludes his account in the *Generall Historie* with a pardonable boast:

'I say only this ... peruse the Spanish decades [ten-part writings], the relations of Master Hakluyt, and tell me how many ever, with such small means as a barge of two tons, sometimes with seven, eight or nine, but at most with twelve or sixteen men, did ever discover so many fair and navigable rivers, subject so many several kings, people and nations to obedience and contribution, with so little bloodshed.'

13

Things Fall Apart

Having got back with their hard-won supplies, Smith and his men estimated that they now had enough to get them through the winter, and 'the fear of starving was abandoned'. When he first became President, he had instituted military exercises; now he divided the company into work-groups, of 10–15 men, who were supposed to work six hours a day, preparing the soil for planting, building, and making pitch, tar and glass, the rest of the time to be spent 'in pastime and merry exercises' (the last sounding depressingly hearty). More to the point, he informed the assembled company that neither he nor the 30–40 industrious men were prepared to maintain 'a hundred idle varlets' in 'idleness and sloth'. Now that he was in sole charge, he told them (quoting St Paul, II Thessalonians, 3:10 – the whole chapter is relevant), 'you must obey this now for a law, that he that will not work shall not eat'. Furthermore, in case they were in any doubt, he pointed out that the constitution, the letters patent, gave him power over them, with the authority to punish as he thought fit. There would even be a scorecard, to show who had worked more or less. Unfortunately, however sensible, this was not a policy likely in the short term to produce general enthusiasm and popularity.

Meanwhile the supposed Dutch house-builders began to find that the supply of tools and arms had slowed to a trickle; Franz came back to find out why, at a meeting arranged at the glass-house about a mile from Jamestown, and possibly even to ambush Smith. Somehow Smith found out, and went out with a party of 20 men to scour the woods and catch him; returning alone, he encountered Wowinchopunck, the werowance of the Paspaheghs, 'a most strong, stout savage'. After a brief, unconvincing display of friendliness, Wowinchopunck suddenly raised his bow and tried to shoot him. Smith closed to grapple with him, and tried to draw his falchion, which Wowinchopunck prevented. As they struggled, they fell into the river, the shorter man in greater danger of being drowned. The Indian now saw two Polish workmen approaching along the bank, and tried to get away, which gave Smith his chance to grab his long hair and throttle him; having got him down and thrashing in the water, Smith drew his falchion, threatening to behead him, until he begged for his life. Struggling up out of the river, he was marched off by the Poles to be chained up in Jamestown jail.

Back in the fort, the search party had returned with Franz as their prisoner; interrogated by Smith, he claimed that he did not know enough English either properly to understand or make himself understood. For all that, he claimed that Powhatan had forced him and the others to stay, threatening their lives, and that, when intercepted he 'was only walking in the woods to gather walnuts'. Like Wowinchopunck, he 'went by the heels', that is, into irons. Now Smith got his prisoners to send messages to Werocomoco, but was told that the Dutchmen would not come back, that Powhatan was not holding them and could not make them go, and that his messengers could not bring them back by force.

While this was going on, Wowinchopunck's family visited him daily with food supplies, which he employed as bribes to enable his escape. Captain Winne set off with a small party in pursuit, but had to fight off Paspahegh warriors, exchanging 'volleys of shot for flights of arrows'. Smith then got hold of two Indians known as 'the most exact villains in the country, Kemps and Tassore', whom he sent as guides for Winne, Percy and 50 more men to recapture their escaped prisoner. He later claimed that his instructions were not followed; at any rate, the raid was bungled, so that at dawn the Indians were gathered in force, derisively calling to them to come ashore and fight. Shots were then exchanged with no injury to anyone; the Indians withdrew, Winne landed, burned Wowinchopunck's house, captured two canoes, and came back. Exasperated, Smith went out on a punitive raid himself, and soon had shot half a dozen, captured an equal number, burned a village and taken away more canoes and fishing lines for use at Jamestown.

On the way back, the Indians shot at his boat, and then revealed themselves, taunting him 'in bravest manner'; when he went for them, they recognised him and threw down their arms. Their spokesman then said that their attack had been directed at Captain Winne, not him. If Smith had been angered by Wowinchopunck's escape, he should remember that even 'the fishes swim, the fowls fly and the very beasts strive to escape the snare and live', and that Wowinchopunck had saved his life before, when he was a prisoner. Furthermore, if Smith continued to destroy their homes and crops, they could easily move away, but the colonists needed their harvests to live. Smith took the point: enough punishment had been done, and he agreed to peace – on condition that provisions were still available.

Back in Jamestown, he found that Master Sicklemore had returned with 'little hope and less certainty' of any Roanoke survivors; Nathanael Powell and reliable Anas Todkill were sent off, three days' journey to the southwest, into Sioux territory, but again in vain. Another old sore started to run again: Indian theft. The Chickahominies' stealing had become excessive: a pistol had been stolen. Two brothers were suspected; one was sent off to retrieve the pistol, the other imprisoned with the threat of being hanged if the gun were not returned within 12 hours. 'Pitying the poor naked savage in the dungeon', Smith had him sent food, and charcoal for a fire; when the brother returned in time with the pistol (Smith was thought to be a man of his word), it was to find that the prisoner, unconscious from the fumes in the closed room, had managed to burn himself severely, and was apparently dead. The survivor lamented with 'such bitter agonies' that Smith promised that, if he swore not to steal any more, he would restore his brother to life. Large quantities of brandy and vinegar were administered, which brought him round, but 'so drunk and affrighted that he seemed lunatic, the which as much tormented and grieved the other as before to see him dead'. Smith then took the poor man away and put him to rest and sleep by a warm fire; in the morning, his burns were treated, and the pair sent off, each with a piece of copper, 'so well contented, that this was spread among all the savages for a miracle, that Captain Smith could make a man alive that was dead'. For some time after this, the Indians round about returned many stolen items (even from Orapaks, Powhatan's new capital), and thieves were even sent to Jamestown to be punished; even better, 'all the country became absolute as free for us as for themselves'.

Under the new régime, conditions seemed slowly to be getting better in Jamestown, and some work was getting done: within three months, in the spring of 1609, six or more tons of tar, pitch and soap-ashes had been made. The glass-house produced some glass; a well was dug in the fort (but still not with as fresh water as had been hoped), the church roof was repaired again, several houses were built, and a blockhouse was constructed on the narrow isthmus connecting Jamestown island to the mainland, to control incoming natives and outgoing thieves. More fishing-nets and lines were set up, there was a large flock of (largely self-supporting) chickens, 30 to 40 acres of land were dug and planted, and another blockhouse begun over the way, on Hog Island, with a small garrison to watch out for unwelcome visitors. Work started on another fort on a little hill two miles inland, 'very hard to be assaulted and easy to be defended'.

What halted all this activity was the discovery that the corn in the storehouse had rotted from the damp and been gnawed and eaten by the swarms of rats that had come over on the ships, so that 'the hogs would scarcely eat it'. Suddenly, the colonists were at their 'wits' end' as to how to get enough to survive: no more could be extorted from the natives. The Indians Kemps and Tassore, who had stayed working in the fields near Jamestown, were released, but, surprisingly, stayed on to help for over two weeks, bringing in with their friends supplies of squirrels, turkeys and deer. It was time for desperate measures.

To reduce the pressure on Jamestown itself, Smith sent about one-third of the colony, under Ensign Laxon, downriver, to catch oysters and whatever else they could get; another score went with Lieutenant Percy to Point Comfort, to live by fishing, but, such was their foolish, idle bickering, 'in six weeks they would not agree to cast out the net, he being sick and burnt sore with gunpowder'. Another group went upriver with Francis West to the falls, to make do with nuts and berries, and the odd squirrel. Some were even billeted among friendly natives, learning from them how to gather and use fruits and plants as they did; under Smith, the English 'had such commanding power ... they durst not wrong us'.

The energetic colonists, however, caught 'more sturgeon than could be devoured by dog or man', some of which they dried and powdered with herbs or roots to make bread. Still, over a hundred remained resentfully unwilling to fend for themselves: 'had they not been forced, *nolens, volens*, perforce to gather and prepare their victuals, they would all have starved or have eaten one another'. Some even went to stay with Kemps, hoping to live off his labours; instead, he continued with Smith's policy, making them choose to work or do without, 'till they were near starved indeed', before he brought them back to Smith.

Many of these 'distracted, gluttonous loiterers' wanted Smith to sell kettles, tools, iron, swords, guns and gunpowder to buy Indian corn – which, of course, he was unwilling to do. At last he agreed to buy half a basket of corn from Powhatan, but to get the other half, he wrote, 'they would have sold their souls'; there were wild demands, as before, to leave the country. Having punished the ringleader, a gentleman named William Dyer, Smith lectured the rest: they should not believe that he intended to starve them, or that Powhatan would feed them. 'If I find any more runners for Newfoundland with the pinnace, let him assuredly look to arrive at the gallows.' Everyone would work to gather food, and feed the sick equally, as he did. 'He that gathereth not every day as much as I do, the next day shall be set beyond the river, and be banished from the fort as a drone, till he amend his conditions or starve.' There were complaints of his cruelty, but, as he wrote later, of approximately 200 colonists, only seven died of starvation or disease during this difficult time.

As it drew towards an end, he decided to send a Swiss, William Volda, to persuade the other runaway foreigners to return, with a promise of pardon: their labours would be needed soon. Unfortunately, Volda revolted, and planned with the others to destroy the colony, the idea being that, with the colonists so dispersed, they could, with Powhatan's help, attack and destroy the fort, seize the pinnace, and bring any survivors back to serve Powhatan. Volda even smuggled out weapons needed for the attack. However, two of the men 'whose Christian hearts relented at such an unChristian act' informed Smith, who told them to keep quiet, but to bring the Dutchmen and Indians to where he might ambush them, so that 'not many of them should return'. When his colleagues were informed, they insisted that only the original plotters should be punished: Lieutenant Percy and Master Cudlington, 'two gentlemen of as bold, resolute spirits as could possibly be found', even volunteered to go and cut their throats, right in Powhatan's face. In the event, Richard Wiffin and Sergeant Abbot were sent to execute them, but the men pleaded for their lives so well that Abbot relented, even though Wiffin was willing 'to stab them or shoot them'. Powhatan kept clear of trouble, sending messages to the effect that he had known nothing of the business, and that he was neither detaining nor maintaining the Dutchmen, nor preventing anyone from carrying out Smith's commands.

Then, in mid-July, all this deadly to-and-fro machination was abruptly interrupted, by the wholly unexpected arrival of a ship, fortunately an English ship (that had actually frightened off a Spanish ship reconnoitring in Chesapeake Bay). She bore food and wine, most welcome in the short term, and, more important in the long term, news of great changes to come.

The ship's captain, Samuel Argall, who at the time was more interested in fishing for sturgeon, presented President Smith with a letter from the London Council, which, apart from reproving him for 'hard dealing with the savages, and not returning the ships freighted' with profitable goods, informed him that another, large supply fleet was on the way. Argall could not tell him much more, as he had left England on 5 May, before all the decisions had been made.

What had happened was that the many reports to London, from Newport, Wingfield, Archer, Ratcliffe, Smith and others, had enforced a review of the whole enterprise. Two points emerged: the southerly crossing took too long (so Argall was sent to develop a shorter, quicker crossing), and, more important, the structure of government needed changing, replacing the president and council system by a single Governor and subordinate council, supervising more colonists. Greater financial backing was needed, which could only be obtained by subscription to a joint stock fund. Word got out, and the scheme took off to an extraordinary degree: the Spanish ambassador, Don Pedro de Zuñiga, who had long kept an unhappy eye on Virginian developments, reported that by the end of February 1609, 14 noblemen had subscribed 40,000 ducats.

The promoters realised the importance of good publicity, and various promotional tracts soon appeared. One, Robert Gray's *A Good Speed to Virginia*, reassured readers that the natives, though 'savage and incredibly rude', were 'by nature loving and gentle, and desirous to embrace a better condition', so that there would be no need for Spanish-type cruelty and repression; furthermore, the natives were 'willing to entertain us, and have offered to yield into our hands on reasonable conditions more land than we shall be able this long time to plant and manure', so that the colonists' land would be obtained 'by lawful grant'. Another tract promised 'houses to live in, vegetable gardens and orchards and also food and clothing' at the expense of the Company, for the 'workmen of whatever craft they may be, blacksmiths, carpenters, coopers, shipwrights, turners and such as know how to plant vineyards, hunters, fishermen ... men as well as women ... who wish to go out in this voyage for colonising the country with people': the kind of people Smith had asked for – if not in such quantity. Within three months, there were over 650 individual subscribers, many city companies, and over 500 volunteers for colonisation and the good life.

Apart from the desire to make money at the expense of the Spanish, James would have been pleased, given the constant nagging of the Spanish ambassador about infringement of Spanish rights, to transfer official responsibility for Virginian colonisation to a private company. So it was agreed: Thomas West, Lord De La Warr, with experience in the Netherlands and Ireland, was named as Lord Governor and Captain General for South Virginia, with the kind of powers that Smith had wished for (but lacked the social status ever to have been granted). His substitute, until His Lordship arrived, was to be Sir Thomas Gates, who had accompanied Drake to the 'rescue' of the Roanoke colonists; Sir Thomas Smythe was to be Treasurer; Sir George Somers was to be Admiral of the Fleet, so demoting Newport (still bobbing along) to vice-admiral; Sir Thomas Dale was to be High Marshal, the military commander. Smith was to stay on the council, but shunted sideways out of the way and put in charge of a fort to be built downriver on Point Comfort. Argall and consequently Smith were not aware of all these appointments, which was to cause further trouble when the fleet at last arrived.

So, on 8 June, the nine ships of the 'third supply' left England. Gates, Somers and Newport each had a copy of the new constitution, and were supposed to travel on different ships; characteristically and sadly predictably, they immediately quarrelled over precedence, and so all travelled on the same ship, the *Sea Venture*, so nullifying the Company's precautions. Newport took the fleet on his familiar southern route, so bringing them into the heat of the tropics in mid-summer: on one ship, 32 died of heatstroke; two babies were born, and died. Then, as they passed the Bahamas, a violent hurricane struck them. William Box wrote in the *Generall Historie* how 'some lost their masts, some their sails blown from their yards; the seas so over-raking our ships, much of our provision was spoiled, our fleet separated, and our men sick and many died.'

William Strachey later wrote a harrowing account of this tempest (as Shakespeare was to call it), how, only a few days' sailing from Point Henry, on 14 July, 'a dreadful storm and hideous began to blow ... which swelling and roaring ... did beat all light from heaven, which like an hell of darkness turned black on us …. our sails, bound up, lay without their use … it could not be said to rain; the waters like whole rivers did flood in the air … here the glut of water, as if throttling the wind erewhile, was no sooner a little emptied and qualified but instantly the winds … spake more loud and grew more tumultuous and malignant … there was not a moment in which the sudden splitting or instant oversetting of the ship was not expected.' When the storm had died down, four ships limped into Chesapeake Bay; no-one knew what had become of the *Sea Venture* and the others.

A look-out saw the fleet, and reported them as a Spanish flotilla; Smith and his men prepared to fight them – even the Indians were ready to join in and ally themselves against the old enemy. Fortunately, they were recognised in time; unfortunately for Smith, among the first individuals he recognised was his old enemy, Gabriel Archer; John Martin was also there. A few days later, another ship arrived, bearing John Ratcliffe; another badly damaged ship got in a few days later.

These were the men of whom Smith had warned, that if they returned, 'they are sufficient to keep us always in factions'. Finding Gates and the others not yet arrived, they began 'so exclaiming against Captain Smith that they [the other newcomers] mortally hated him ere ever they saw him', and demanded he forthwith resign his position. Smith of course refused: there were no documents to confirm the new government and the end of his presidency – and he knew what these men were like.

Confusion, argument and counter-argument ran riot: 'To a thousand mischiefs these lewd captains led this lewd company, wherein were many unruly gallants, packed thither by their friends to escape ill destinies.' Smith complained of the 'infinite dangers, plots and practices he daily escaped'. Ratcliffe and Martin even 'chose' – without any authority – De La Warr's younger brother, Francis West, to be Governor, with the condition he should not 'disturb the old President during his time, but as his authority expired'. In the event, Smith remained President, by virtue of the original Royal charter.

Work still had to be done – more housing (there were women and children in the new supply), harvesting and trading for corn: winter had to be prepared for. Repeating his strategy of the previous winter, Smith divided the colony into separate groups. One was sent with Francis West to the falls area again. Fed up with the whole business, Smith offered the presidency to John Martin, who accepted and then immediately declined it, instead taking another party, of some 60 men, to the Nansemond River area. Taking an over-aggressive approach, things went badly there, as he surprised 'the poor naked king' (it is remarkable how Smith's epithets for the natives changed) and occupied his house and island, thus provoking a vigorous counter-attack that killed two colonists and carried off the captive chief and 1,000 bushels of corn. Martin sent to Smith for reinforcements, but did nothing useful with them.

Smith had gone upriver, to inspect the falls settlement, meeting – to his surprise – West on his way down. The camp he found set too near the river and in danger of flooding, so sent a message to Parahunt offering to buy the nearby village of Powhatan, as an outpost against the Monacan threat, in return for copper, with various additional provisos about tribute payments and punishments of thieves. The chief agreed, but the newcomers mutinously refused. Smith landed at the camp with his five men and attempted to bring it to order, but was forced to 'retire' by the 120. He spent nine days trying to persuade them that they were mistaken in their 'great gilded hopes of the South Sea mines' and other promises; instead, they tormented 'the poor savages' by 'stealing their corn, robbing their gardens, beating them, breaking their houses and keeping some prisoners', so that the Indians complained that they were worse than the Monacans.

No sooner had he set off back for Jamestown than the Indians attacked the men, 'slew many' and rescued their prisoners. His boat having gone aground on a mudbank, Smith went back, to find the unhappy campers 'amazed with this poor silly assault of twelve savages', as he contemptuously phrased it. He took command, arrested six or seven leading trouble-makers, made peace with the Indians, and moved the party into Powhatan village with its ready-made defences, 'sufficient

to have defended them from all the savages in Virginia, dry houses for
lodgings and near two hundred acres of ground ready to be planted, and
no place [he] knew so strong, so pleasant and delightful in Virginia, for
which we called it Nonsuch' (after Queen Elizabeth's favourite palace, at
Richmond in Surrey).

No sooner was all apparently settled than West returned, to find his
camp displaced and his people in uproarious complaint against Smith.
George Percy later wrote how he had heard that 'a great division did grow
amongst them [Smith and De La Warr's brother and 'president-elect'].
Captain Smith, perceiving both his authority and person neglected',
then, according to Percy, incited the Indians to attack the colonists, a
charge that tells one more about the accusers than the accused. West
moved his people back to 'West's Fort', such as it was, and the angry
Captain Smith took his boat back for Jamestown.

Resting in the boat with his five companions, he dozed off. Somehow,
a spark or flame, perhaps from one of the matches always kept burning
for the muskets, perhaps from a tobacco pipe, fell on the pouch of gunpowder strapped to his side, which exploded into flame, 'which tore the
flesh from his body and thigh, nine or ten inches square, in a most pitiful
manner; but to quench the tormenting fire frying him in his clothes, he
leapt overboard into the deep river, where, ere they could recover him,
he was near drowned. In this state, without either surgeon or surgery, he
was to go near a hundred miles.'

His condition on his return to Jamestown can readily be imagined;
still, weakened as he was, he tried to make fresh arrangements for obtaining provisions. He heard that, seeing he was 'unable to stand, and near
bereft of his senses by reason of his torment', Archer and some others
'had plotted to have him murdered in his bed', but that the chosen assas-
sin had lost heart. They then attempted to take over the government, and
his friends urged him 'to take their heads'. Instead, ill and weary, he sent
for the masters of the ships to arrange for his passage back to England.
This was the cue for Ratcliffe, Archer and Martin to make another move.
They immediately met to decide who was now to rule, but, unable to

agree, had to settle for persuading George Percy, who had been unwell and intending to go back, to stay on as President. Smith, now on board ship, wrote only that he would never have agreed to transfer the government to them, but 'was not unwilling that they should steal it'. They followed up by getting anyone he had offended or punished to combine in preparing an indictment against him (Archer was always keen on the forms of law). Complaints included accusations from the mutineers at the falls that Smith had got the natives to attack them, from the Dutch traitors that he had tried to poison them, from survivors that he had made them collect oysters, and that he had wanted to marry Pocahontas in order to become king.

Before the ship sailed, Ratcliffe gave one of the ships' captains a letter for the Earl of Salisbury, that reported the assumed loss of the *Sea Venture* and all on board, and complained that Smith had not treated the newcomers with respect, being now 'sent home to answer some misdemeanours, whereof I persuade me he can scarcely clear himself from great imputation of blame.' Finally, he observed that it was hard work clearing wooded ground for planting, and a year's food supply would be very welcome.

By now, Smith's term of office had expired; the last of Gates's fleet had struggled in, except the *Sea Venture*, so Percy stayed on as President. On 4 October 1609, John Smith left Virginia, never to return. He left behind over 500 colonists, most of them newcomers who knew little of how to live there or of what he had done. One long-term colonist who did, William Fettiplace (who has a marvellous memorial in Swinbrook Church, Oxfordshire), wrote: 'What shall I say? But thus we lost him, that in all his proceedings made justice his first guide, and experience his second; ever hating baseness, sloth, pride and indignity more than any dangers; that never allowed more for himself than his soldiers with him; that upon no danger would send them where he would not lead them himself; that would never see us want what either he had or could by any means get us ... whose adventures were our lives, and whose loss our deaths.'

14

Since You've Been Gone

As Smith was accused of mismanagement, it is worth reviewing how the colony got on without him. News of his departure quickly reached Powhatan, who promptly initiated what is sometimes called the First Anglo-Powhatan War (1609–14), with a violent attack, when, as the *Generall Historie* recorded, the natives 'all revolted, and did murder and spoil [plunder] all they could encounter'. John Martin, who had been at Nansemond, came back to Jamestown, leaving Michael Sicklemore in charge; as Indian attacks continued, 17 men also fled the camp in a boat. They were never heard of again. Sicklemore and some others then went to trade for food; their bodies were found later, their mouths mockingly stuffed with bread. After a series of attacks on Francis West's fort at the falls, he and his men also pulled back to Jamestown. Ratcliffe stayed on in the new fort being built downriver at Point Comfort.

The colony was once again in a bad situation: stores had been consumed (there were many more mouths to feed), and the fishing-nets were rotten. Now Powhatan sent a tempting present of venison, followed by an invitation to visit and trade. With alacrity, Percy sent Ratcliffe in a ship to visit Powhatan at his new headquarters at Orapaks. Once there, Ratcliffe failed to exchange hostages (something Smith had always made a point of doing); leaving some men in the ship commanded by William Fettiplace, he and his men spent the night ashore, before beginning trading, copper and beads for corn. As often, different accounts of what happened differ slightly; there was a dispute, and Ratcliffe's men were ambushed on their way back to the ship, and killed. He himself was captured, and received the same treatment as George Cassen, this time by women, as his skin was scraped off with mussel shells and burned before his eyes, before he himself was burned alive. 'And so,' wrote Percy, all heart, 'for want of circumspection [he] miserably perished.' The Indians, unusually, followed up with an attack on the ship, and were only repelled with difficulty. The ship returned with no corn, and only 16 men alive of the original 50.

Now Percy sent Francis West and another large party to trade with the Patawomecks, a relatively distant tribe who therefore might be well disposed. In practice, West and his men behaved as badly as they had done before, and, as Percy admitted, 'used some harsh and cruel dealings, by cutting off two of the savages' heads and other extremities'. The ship was then loaded with a good supply of corn. Astonishingly, when the ship reached Point Comfort, where Captain Davis 'did call unto them ... exhorting them to make all the speed they could to relieve us', instead of turning into the James River, West and his men hoisted more sail and made for the open sea, and England. One might have thought this disgraceful treachery inexcusable and worthy of punishment – but West had Lord De La Warr, the new Lord Governor of Virginia, as a brother; instead, he was later given command of another vessel, to return to Virginia.

Now began what became known as 'the Starving Time', when, as one contributor to Smith's *Generall Historie* wrote, 'Now we all found the want of Captain Smith; yea, his greatest maligners could then curse his loss.' Powhatan continued his starvation strategy, killing all the pigs on Hog Island, and attacking any colonists who left the shelter of Jamestown Fort. Some men robbed the dwindling stocks in the storehouse and were executed. Others turned to eating the colony's chickens, horses, dogs and cats; then the rats – there were still plenty – mice and snakes. Roots, herbs and nuts lasted for a while. Then shoeleather. The starch used to stiffen their ruffs made a sort of porridge. Cannibalism loomed; after an Indian was killed in an attack and buried, he was dug up and eaten. One man killed his pregnant wife, dropped the foetus into the river, chopped her up, salted the pieces and ate some before he was discovered and executed. A writer in the *Generall Historie* indulged in grimly callous humour: 'now whether she was better roasted, boiled or carbonadoed [grilled] I know not, but of such a dish as powdered [salted] wife I never heard of.' Despair ruled: Percy recorded a colonist 'crying out that there was no God, alleging that if there were a God He would not suffer His creatures, whom He made and framed, to endure those miseries, and to perish for want of food and sustenance.' Later, the man went out into the woods to find something to eat; his body was found shot through with arrows and partly eaten by animals.

It was all due to sheer incompetence on the part of Percy, Martin, West and the other leaders, alienating every native tribe and failing to organise their own supplies. When Percy at last got round to visiting the men at Point Comfort, he found them all well: they had been living on shellfish and their own pigs, unaware of difficulties elsewhere. By March 1610, there were only some 60 of the original colonists in Jamestown still alive.

At this desperately low point, the look-outs at Point Comfort saw two small vessels approaching; amazingly, their crews were the survivors of the *Sea Venture*, long thought drowned. William Strachey reported what had happened. The ship had been severely damaged in the tempest, so much so that they had to throw overboard their cannon and most of their supplies, food and drink. Exhausted, they were about to give up, when Sir George Somers saw land, and they were able to run the ship onto coral shallows, three-quarters of a mile from the shore. 150 men, women and children had landed on the Bermudas, dreaded as the 'Devil's Islands' for their storms and rocky shoals. Here they survived; eventually Somers got a shipbuilder to construct a new craft from the remains of the old, and Bermudan timber, and took responsibility for building a smaller craft himself. Despite rebellions from those unwilling to risk leaving Bermuda, the *Deliverance* and *Patience* were at last ready. On 10 May a westerly wind took them to sea, and then to Point Comfort on 22 May.

George Percy, still there (shellfish, pork and safety in the fort), would have given the new Governor some idea of the situation in Jamestown, but it was still a shock when they got there two days later. Strachey relates how, 'viewing the fort, we found the palisades torn down, the ports open, the gates from off the hinges, and empty houses (which owners' deaths had taken from them) rent up and burnt, rather than the dwellers would step into the woods a stone's cast off from them to fetch other firewood. And it is true, the Indians killed as fast without, if our men stirred but beyond the bounds of their blockhouse, as famine and pestilence did within.'

The situation was hopeless: there was no food, except the little the new arrivals had brought with them, and apparently no means of getting more; the natives were (very) hostile; morale had collapsed. Powhatan had won. The importance of John Smith, in imposing discipline on the colonists and respect from the natives, and ensuring food supplies, could not be more clearly demonstrated. Gates decided to abandon the colony as soon as the four craft they now had could be made ready, and head north to the Newfoundland fishing grounds, where English fishing boats might help them back to England. The announcement was met, wrote Strachey, with 'a general acclamation and shout of joy'.

On the morning of 7 June, everything was ready. Some men wanted to burn down the buildings, but Gates refused, as they might be useful in the future. They sailed at noon, and spent the night off Hog Island. The next morning, approaching Point Comfort, they were, unexpectedly, intercepted by a ship's longboat. It brought a letter for Gates: a new fleet was in the offing, and a new Governor, who had been told by the remnant at Point Comfort of the situation – and they should wait, which, 'to the great grief of all his [Gates's] company', they did.

What had happened, in brief, was that Smith had got back to London by the end of December 1609, about six weeks after Samuel

Argall, so that the London Council was soon fully informed of the dissension, disorder and incoherent governance in Jamestown. There is no record whatever of Smith being in any trouble with the Council, whatever his enemies had written. Instead, the Council published pamphlets intended to reassure investors, explain away the disappearance of the *Sea Venture* and insist that the Company had everything in hand: Lord De La Warr was going out, with vice-regal powers, as Lord Governor and Captain General. Three ships set sail on 1 April, with 150 new colonists, but without Captain Smith – perhaps because he was still convalescing, perhaps because it was felt he would not 'fit in'. At all events, here was the new man, sailing upriver, and determined to sort things out.

A contemporary writer for the Company, in *A True Declaration*, saw divine providence at work in all this: 'For if God had not sent Sir Thomas Gates from the Bermudas within four days, they had been all famished. If God had not directed the heart of that worthy knight to save the fort from fire at their shipping, they had been destitute of a present harbour and succour. If they had abandoned the fort any longer time and had not so returned, questionless the Indians would have destroyed the fort, which had been the means of our safety among them, and a terror unto them. If they had set sail sooner and had launched into the vast ocean, who could have promised that they should have encountered the fleet of Lord La-Ware? – especially when they made for Newfoundland, a course contrary to our navy's approaching. If the Lord La-Ware had not brought with him a year's provision, what comfort could those souls have received to have been relanded to a second destruction?'

Arriving in Jamestown on Sunday, 10 June, De La Warr (hereinafter West) found the place stinking and dirty, 'occasioned much by the mortality and idleness of our own people'. After a sermon, and a formal transfer of authority from Gates, West spent a few crisp words on the assembled company, 'laying some blames upon them for haughty vanities and sluggish idleness', with a threat to 'draw the sword in justice to cut off delinquents'. Everyone – including soft-handed gentlemen – would be set to work, six hours a day. The next day, he ordered the general filth and rubbish cleared away, and on the Wednesday convened his new council, including Gates, Somers and Percy. The first problem was the food supply: surprisingly, Somers volunteered to take the *Patience* back to Bermuda, to bring back fish and some of the wild hogs there, taking with him Argall in the *Discovery*. (Once again, a storm trapped the party on the islands, and while they were there, Somers, aged 56, thought a good age then, died 'of a surfeit of eating of a pig'.)

The next problem was of relations with the natives. The London Council had hoped to win them over to peace and Christianity, especially by getting rid of their priests, but when Gates saw one of his men captured and killed by a party of Kecoughtans, peaceful methods were discontinued. A few days later he drew the Kecoughtans out of cover by having a taborer play his drum and fife in front of them; his men ambushed them, killed five and wounded many others. West at first tried a different tactic, sending messengers to Powhatan demanding the return of stolen tools and weapons and any prisoners he had, in exchange for renewed friendship. Powhatan replied with 'proud and disdainful answers': the English should stay in Jamestown or leave the country, or be killed at leisure; the messengers should not return except with a present of a coach and three horses.

West responded by sending a force under Percy to the Paspahegh village, where they killed Wowinchopunck and several men, burned the village and carried off the Paspaheghs' queen and her children. On the way back, Percy and his men decided to kill the children by throwing them overboard and shooting them. Back in Jamestown he got Captain Davis to ask West what he wanted done about the queen; Davis reported that West wanted her 'despatched', preferably by being burned alive; to give her a quicker end, Percy had Davis and two men take her ashore and 'put her to the sword'. So much for criticism of Smith's severity towards the natives.

Later, West complained that, on arriving at Jamestown, he was struck by an ague, and then other illnesses, before 'the flux surprised [him]', then cramp and gout. In March, 1611, he sailed off with Gates,

Newport, Strachey and several others, first for the West Indies and then for England; hard graft in Virginia was not for His Lordship – someone else would have to do the job.

For a while the colony was led by George Percy (described by West as 'a gentleman of honour and resolution') and by Gates, back again. Then, in May, 1611 Sir Thomas Dale arrived as deputy governor to Gates, an ex-soldier from the Netherlands and the hard man's hard man. When he arrived at Jamestown, 'most of the company were at their usual works, bowling in the streets'. In no time they were chopping timber, sowing and repairing rotten housing and the fencing. Under his revision of the colony's laws, execution became the penalty for adultery (no longer a merely theoretical fantasy – there were now several women colonists), as well as for theft, however petty, and unauthorised trading with the natives. Those who were late for work were to be whipped, as were those who did 'the necessities of nature' within a quarter of a mile of the fort, and anyone who criticised the administration.

A major concern of the Company had always been the establishment of a secure inland fort, away from marauding Spanish ships. After a scare when a Spanish caravel arrived off Point Comfort and kidnapped a man, there was a more determined effort to develop an inland site. That September, Gates sent Dale with 300 men to build a fort on high, open ground, in a defensible position, with access to fresh water, in a bend of the James River, near the village of Arrohattock, to be called Henrico. Winter cold came on early that year, but before any shelters could be built, seven acres of land had to be properly fenced in within ten days, and five high, strong watchtowers and storage huts constructed. Security was the absolute priority, before the men could build any shelters.

Jacobeans were used to strict laws and punishments, but there was shocked comment (by 'Ancient Planters of Virginia' in *A Brief Declaration*, 1624) of how Dale 'oppressed his whole company with ... extraordinary labours by day, and watching by night ... ', of how 'want of houses at first landing in the cold of winter, and pinching hunger continually biting, made those imposed labours most insufferable, and the best fruits and effects thereof to be no better than the slaughter of His Majesty's subjects by starving, hanging, burning, breaking upon the wheel and shooting to death. Some, more than half famished, running to the Indians to get relief, being again returned, were burnt to death.' Those who tried to escape in a shallop and barge were shot, hanged and broken on the wheel. The daily ration, it was reported, was 'but nine ounces of corrupt and putrefied meal and half a pint of oatmeal or peas, of like ill condition'.

Ralph Hamor's defence of Dale was that he had not been 'tyrannous, nor severe at all': some might consider his executions 'cruel, unusual and barbarous', but the French and other countries did much the same. Terror was the most effective technique, 'it being true that amongst those people, who for the most part are sensible only of the body's torment, the fear of a cruel, painful and unusual death more restrains than death itself'. Dale was indeed severe; but discipline was essential if the colony were to survive. Henrico fort was built: in 1614, there were three streets of frame houses, a church and brick foundations for a larger church. However, it was in a poor state in 1616, and by 1619, practically abandoned.

It was not all ruthless brutality; there was some intelligence. There was a policy of alliance with those not subordinate to the Powhatan empire, notably the Patawomecks on the south side of the Potomac River. Samuel Argall had originally been hired as a transatlantic ferryman, but became a useful and trusted trading intermediary with the natives. In March 1613, exploring along the Potomac, he learnt that Pocahontas, now perhaps 15 or so, was staying with the Patawomecks, and decided to kidnap her, as a hostage in exchange for English prisoners, arms and tools. Having been told that Smith was dead, she had not been seen at Jamestown, and, according to William Strachey, married at the age of puberty in 1610 'a private [native] captain' named Kocoum (there is no other reference to him; Indian divorce was easy, and not uncommon). In any case, she was not living with her father or his people, but a little way off, with the Patawomecks.

Argall was on good terms with the chief, Japazeus, 'an old friend of Captain Smith', and told him that he must get Pocahontas for him, promising both that he would not hurt her, and to give him a fine copper kettle. Japazeus and his wife brought Pocahontas to the river bank to look at Argall's ship, and persuaded her to go on board with them. Argall then gave them supper in the cabin, after which they spent the night on board. In the morning, she was first up and anxious to be away; however, Argall told her she would have to stay, at which 'she began to be exceeding pensive and discontented'. Japazeus and his wife went off with their copper kettle and some other items, 'so highly by him esteemed that doubtless he would have betrayed his own father for them', wrote Hamor, contemptuously.

Argall then sent a message to Powhatan, demanding the return of eight English prisoners and the weapons and tools he had stolen, in exchange for his daughter. There was no immediate response, but eventually Powhatan sent seven Englishmen, each with a musket, and a promise of 500 bushels of corn; he was informed that his daughter was safe in Henrico, but the remaining materials were still required. In March 1614 Dale impatiently took 150 men (and Pocahontas) up the Pamunkey River, demanding the weapons and corn; after a skirmish, they burned 40 houses and killed five or six braves. Eventually, negotiations began; two of her brothers came to see that she was well, but, to their surprise, Miss was on her dignity. Her view was that her father apparently valued her less than old swords and guns, 'wherefore she would still dwell with the Englishmen, who loved her'.

The Englishmen who loved her included not only the Revd Alexander Whitaker, who had instructed her in Christianity, but one John Rolfe, a 28-year-old widower, survivor of the *Sea Venture* and enthusiastic planter of West Indian tobacco (much superior to the local strain). Now he wrote a nervous letter to Dale, expressing his feelings and asking permission to marry her (Dale had complete authority, it was not a good idea to displease him, and the proposed match had obvious, major political implications).

The letter is a wonderful illustration of Puritan anxieties. He had been, he wrote, very agitated at coming 'to be in love with one whose educa-tion hath been so rude, her manners barbarous, her generation cursed, and so discrepant in all nutriture' from himself. He was, he insisted, 'no way led (so far forth as man's weakness may permit) with the unbridled desire of carnal affection, but for the good of this plantation, for the honour of our country, for the glory of God, for mine own salvation and for the converting to the true knowledge of God and Jesus Christ an unbelieving creature, namely Pocahontas. To whom my hearty and best thoughts have a long time been so entangled and enthralled in so intri-cate a labyrinth, that I was even a-wearied to unwind myself thereout. But Almighty God ... hath opened the gate and led me by the hand, that I might plainly see and discern the safest path wherein to tread.'

Perish the thought that he was sexually drawn to an attractive, intel-ligent young woman; 'the many passions and sufferings' he had endured, even in his sleep, 'awaking [him] to astonishment', were wholly religious impulses, directing him to his duty as a Christian, to convert her and 'labour in the Lord's vineyard, there to sow and plant ... to the comfort of the labourer in this life, and his salvation in the world to come.' The 'lab-yrinth' reference indicates Rolfe's memory of reading in school the story of Theseus and the Minotaur. Pocahontas/Ariadne, the young woman to be saved, should provide the guiding thread through the labyrinth for Rolfe/Theseus, entangled in fears of the imaginary Minotaur, the embodiment of sacrilegious cross-cultural sexual unions (as denounced in Ezra 9:12 and 10:3, to which he alludes); nevertheless, God has helped him to find a way out, probably through Genesis.

Ironically, the marriage about which he was so anxious was an enactment of a favourite metaphor of colonialists, as in Volume XIX of *Purchas his Pilgrimes*: 'Look upon Virginia, view her lovely looks ... worth the wooing and loves of the best husband.' In converting the natives, 'we shall overcome both men and devils, and espouse Virginia to one husband ... if we be careful to do God's will, he will be ready to do ours ... Christian suitors ... there may sow spirituals and reap tem-porals.' Political marriages were a familiar concept for both Europeans and Indians. Dale approved, as did Powhatan. The English returned to Henrico, where Pocahontas was baptised, the first native American to convert to Christianity, under the name of Rebecca. In Genesis 25:23, Rebekah, the wife of Isaac, is told by the Lord, 'Two nations are in thy womb; and two manner of people shall be separated from thy bowels; and the one people shall be stronger than the other people; and the elder shall serve the younger.' Particularly pleasing to the English was that the inferior, Esau, was red and a hunter, and subordinate to the supplanter, Jacob, an indoor man.

On 14 April, the wedding, 'another knot to build this peace the stronger,' in Dale's words, took place, with one of her uncles and two brothers in attendance. Both the English and the Powhatans hoped for peace from this union, and for some time this proved to be the case. 'Ever since,' wrote Hamor, 'we have had friendly commerce and trade not only with Powhatan but also with his subjects round about us.' Indeed, not only did the Chickahominies formally ally themselves with the English, but Dale followed up with proposing to Powhatan that (despite being already married) he should marry one of Pocahontas's even younger half-sisters. The old chief was not having that, and declined wearily, saying she was promised elsewhere, but told Hamor, Dale's emissary, that he had seen 'too many of his men and mine killed, and by my occasion there shall never be more ... . I am old now and would gladly end my days in peace ... Thus much I hope will satisfy my brother. Now, because yourselves are weary and I am sleepy, we will thus end the discourse of this business.'

15

Perplexed Thoughts

On his return to London, Smith would have reported to the Council, which, far from making trouble for him, was busy trying to reassure everyone that all was well, and with organising Lord De La Warr's expedition. He would have been surprised to discover that he was now a published author, his earlier letter having been passed on by its unknown recipient and published under the title, *A true relation of ... occurrences and accidents ... in Virginia ...* . Confusingly, the first title-page asserted only that it had been written 'by a gentleman of the said colony'; next, it was attributed to 'Thomas Watson, Gent., one of the said colony'; then, to 'Captain Smith, Colonel of the said colony', and then at last the initial 'Col' and final 'l' were obliterated. An address to 'the courteous reader', signed I.H., says that the letter has been edited, omitting material thought 'fit to be private' – probably not personal matters, but material unhelpful to Company policy. Indeed, in November 1610 the Company put out a revised puff-pamphlet, *A True declaration of the estate of the Colony in Virginia.*

Smith now turned to providing his own truthful account of Virginia, working with several others who had been there with him – Richard Wiffin (who had told him of Scrivener's drowning), his old supporter Anas Todkill, Richard Potts and others. The book, with the overall title, *A Map of Virginia*, with a fine, accurate map based on Smith's explorations, engraved by William Hole (a distinguished illustrator, who had drawn maps for William Camden's *Britannia*), and pictures of Powhatan and a Susquehanna brave, was in two parts. The first, *The Description of Virginia*, entirely by Smith, provided a detailed description of the land and resources of the Chesapeake Bay area and reasonably accurate accounts of the customs and culture of its people, together with an intriguing list of Indian words and phrases (that in itself implied the difficulties of life for the first colonists). Here for the first time appear in print Indian words that entered the English language, such as 'moccasins', 'hickory' and 'hominy'. His celebration of Virginia – 'Heaven and earth never agreed better to frame a place for man's habitation' – has an implicit criticism of many of the colonists – 'were it fully manured and inhabited by industrious people'. Such criticism was part of the business of the second section, *The Proceedings of the English Colony in Virginia*, consisting of writings by Smith and several others, recounting the events of their early years, edited by Richard Potts. The whole was overseen and edited by the Revd William Symonds ('The pains I took were great'), who had links with Ralegh Crashaw who had been in Virginia, and with Sir Robert Bertie, Lord Willoughby, one of the first that Smith would have looked up on his return.

The Proceedings is partly a defence of the industrious and pro-Smith colonists against the others, justifying its revelations of the various disputes: 'These brawls are so disgustful, as some [such as the Virginia Company] will say they are better forgotten, yet all men of good judgement will conclude, it were better their [the troublemakers'] baseness should be manifest to the world, than the business bear the scorn and shame of their excused disorders.' Indeed, 'happy had we been had they [the riff-raff that came over with De La Warr's party] never arrived, and we for ever abandoned and (as we were) left to our fortunes.' Arrogance and greed for early profits, especially the obsession with gold, had greatly harmed the whole venture.

There may have been difficulties in getting the book printed in London, against the wishes of the great men of the London Company.

Symonds was an Oxford graduate, and may have been helpful in getting the small quarto volume printed there in 1612. It was always important to get high-ranking men behind one in such ventures, and Smith dedicated the volume to Sir Edward Seymour, Earl of Hertford – again someone with links to Sir Robert Bertie. Smith hints that he has had difficulty in getting suitable employment, and could do with some help; as it is, he writes, 'having been discouraged from doing any more, I have writ this little.' It was customary to praise one's patron, in this case the Earl's 'virtue', but Smith's relatively egalitarian feelings (that had caused him trouble in the past) peep through: 'Though riches now be the chiefest greatness of the great, when great and little are born and die, there is no difference: virtue only makes men more than men.'

Smith's own merits were not wholly unrecognised in England. William Strachey, survivor of the *Sea Venture*, inspirer of Shakespeare and secretary of the colony in Virginia, had returned, partly to write up and publish the laws of Virginia. His *Historie of travell into Virginia Britannia*, partly derived from Smith's *Map of Virginia*, was also published in 1612. Strachey got George Percy, newly returned from Virginia (having, like another high-handed scion of noble family, Francis West, 'done a runner' from the colony with a boat, its crew and fish intended for his fellow colonists), to present a copy to his brother, the Earl of Northumberland. In it, he wrote, of Smith, 'Sure I am, there will not return from thence in haste, anyone who hath been more industrious, or who hath had (Captain George Percy excepted) greater experience amongst them, however misconstruction may traduce him here at home, where is not easily seen the mixed sufferances both of body and mind, which is there daily and with no few hazards and hearty griefs undergone.' For all that, as Smith pointed out, he was no better off, with no gentleman's estate to return to: 'my hands hath been my lands this fifteen years, in Europe, Asia, Africa or America.' He had to make his own way, and needed employment for his hands and restless spirit.

At last, in March 1614, a group of investors, led by Marmaduke Rawdon, a London merchant, hired Smith and another captain, Thomas

Hunt, for a new venture, to go whaling and to 'make trials of a mine of gold and copper' – though the latter, as Smith later acknowledged, was really more Hunt's 'device, to get a voyage that projected it, than any knowledge he had at all of any such matter'. As it turned out, the whaling part of the venture did not go well, the whales in the area (off Maine) being unsuitable 'jubartes' (rorqual or finback whales), aggressive and lacking suitable oil. Leaving the others to get on with fishing, Smith took a boat and small crew to survey the coastline. The maps he had he found were useless – 'no more good than so much waste paper' – so he drew a careful and very accurate map, 'from point to point, isle to isle and harbour to harbour, with the soundings, sands, rocks and landmarks, as I passed close aboard the shore in a little boat.' Among the landmarks he recorded were Cape Tragabigzanda, after his admirer back in Turkey, Cape Cod ('Cape James', he named it) and Plymouth ('Accomack') – 'good land, and no want of anything but industrious people' – where he landed some seven years before the Pilgrims. His colleague, Captain Hunt, went to Cape Cod, captured 24 natives and then sold them as slaves in Spain; he also tried, Smith wrote, to steal his maps and notes, 'and so to leave me alone in a desolate isle, to the fury of famine and all other extremities, lest I should have acquainted Sir Thomas Smythe, my honourable good friend, and the Council of Virginia,' in order to take over Smith's plans for a colony in Massachusetts.

In fact, Smith went first to Plymouth, to Sir Ferdinando Gorges of the Plymouth Company, which originally had been entitled to develop northern 'Virginia', to discuss his proposal. The people there approved, granting him authority in 'New England', as he named it (perhaps remembering Drake naming California 'New Albion'), and the title 'Admiral of New England'. He always considered the land he had named, New England, as much his 'child' as the land he had saved, Virginia. There was difficulty in getting enough investors, but at last, largely through his own efforts, enough money was raised and, in the summer of 1615 he got two ships, with orders to bring back fish and whale oil, and to settle a small colony of himself and 16 others, to be relieved or resupplied the next year.

One ship was lost at sea, and his own ship nearly sank, with her masts broken and gear thrown overboard, so that 'only her spritsail remained to spoon before the wind'; they put up a jury rig, and got back somehow.

On 24 June he set off again, in what he calls a 'small bark of sixty tons', with 14 sailors and his original 16 prospective colonists. Soon, however, he was chased for two days by a larger English pirate ship. His ship's officers were eager not to resist for too long, and the pirates were able to close in and get aboard, Smith refusing to come out of his cabin to meet them. Surprisingly, some of them claimed to be former shipmates of his, and offered that, if he would join with them, he could be overall captain of their pirate flotilla; he declined the offer, and they sailed off.

Next, two French pirate ships caught up with him and demanded he give himself up; once again his sailors urged a prompt surrender, fearing enslavement by Turks or being thrown overboard if they resisted. Smith replied that he would blow up and sink the ship rather than surrender. His crew were forced to put up a fight, which they did sufficiently well to get away from the others. A day later, no fewer than four French ships closed in on the luckless Englishmen. Smith now went on board one, to parley, and learned that they were privateers, sailing with letters of marque licensing them to attack Spanish, Portuguese and pirate vessels – but not English ones. The account of what followed is not very clear, but, in brief, the French captain, François Perret, Sieur du Poiron, took over the English ship, its crew, provisions and weapons. More French ships joined the flotilla, pursuing other passing vessels; eventually the men and provisions (but not their weapons) were restored. Smith now wanted to carry on to Virginia, but the others had had enough excitement and wanted only to go home. He went over to Du Poiron's ship to collect some weapons, when a storm blew up. The English shipmaster called to him to come back, but Smith called that he could not make the Frenchmen do what he wanted, and the shipmaster refused to send the ship's boat for him, saying it was split. During the night, the English slipped away, and Smith was left on the French ship, the *Don de Dieu*, alone, in only 'his cap, breeches and waistcoat'.

Du Poiron continued to cruise near the Azores, hoping for prey, while Smith filled his time – September and October – by starting to write a book about his experiences in New England, 'to keep my perplexed thoughts from too much meditation of my miserable estate', as he put it. Du Poiron's piracy had some success, as Smith recorded; in October he seized what Smith called 'a poor carvel of Brazil', laden with 'three hundred and seventy chests of sugar, one hundred hides and thirty thousand reales of eight [the silver "pieces of eight" that Long John Silver's parrot celebrated]'. After another raid, Du Poiron at last kept his promise to release Smith, and put him in the caravel to go to La Rochelle. Despite this, Du Poiron's lieutenant, in charge of the caravel, kept Smith, demanding that he sign a document for the French authorities, clearing him and Du Poiron of any illegal activity. The consequences of his failing to sign were not made explicit, but were easily imagined.

Fortunately for Smith, a storm blew up, requiring the crew's full attention; seizing his opportunity and the ship's boat, towed astern, he set off into the night, 'come wind, come weather', his papers safely wrapped up (every writer will appreciate his care for the manuscript), and a half-pike as a wholly inadequate steering oar, to make for the coast. Currents, winds and tide dragged him this way and that; buffeted by wind and rain, continually baling, the indomitable was swept ashore onto 'an oozy isle by Charowne [the Charente river]'. Came the dawn, the wind driving grey clouds inshore over the mudflats, some men out fowling found him 'near drowned, and half dead with water, cold and hunger'. With their help, and after selling the ship's boat (not strictly his to sell), he got to La Rochelle, where he learned that the *Don de Dieu* and Du Poiron had both gone down in the storm.

There, he went to the Admiralty office, to complain and demand compensation for unlawful detention and loss of property. Not surprisingly, he encountered some resistance from French bureaucracy, but received 'bountiful assistance', he tells us, from a 'Madame Chanoyes at Rochelle', another of his lady benefactors, who arranged for him to meet Sir Thomas Edmondes, the English ambassador, newly come to

Bordeaux to greet the Spanish Infanta on her way to her marriage to Louis XIII. More in hope than expectation, Smith put in for a share of the profits resulting from the capture of the Brazilian ship; there is no evidence that he got any.

Back in Plymouth in December 1615, he found that his former ship-mates who had abandoned him to the mercies of the French had sold and shared out the profits from his clothes, books, weapons and instruments. He soon had them 'laid by the heels'; some went to prison. How much, if any, of his property he recovered is not known.

Smith was not the man to loiter futilely in Plymouth; soon he was back in London, with his manuscript, working his contacts to produce a saleable new propaganda booklet for New England venturers. The *Description of New England* was dedicated to King James's Privy Council, and also to the youthful Prince Charles (heir to the throne since Prince Henry's death), inviting him to accept Smith's excellent new map and 'please to change their barbarous [place-]names for such English, as posterity may say, Prince Charles was their godfather', an offer that was taken up. The map was well drawn, with a portrait of Captain Smith. There were also nine commendatory verses, including one by John Davies of Hereford, poet and former writing-master to Prince Henry, whose line, 'thou art Brasse without, but Golde within,' neatly suggests both his inner quality and his coloration. Published in June 1616, this time in London, only 60 pages long, the book discusses the area Smith had seen from his boat, urging further action: 'more than half is yet unknown'. In particular, this was, unlike England, a land of equal opportunity, where 'every man may be a master and owner of his own labour and land ... . If he have nothing but his hands, he may ... by industry quickly grow rich... . Who can desire more content, that has small means, or but only his merit to advance his fortune, than to tread and plant that ground he hath purchased by the hazard of his life ... ?' It sounds very much like John Smith. In the margin is printed, 'A note for men that have great spirits and small means.'

Early June also saw the arrival in Plymouth of Sir Thomas Dale, to boast of his success in 'the hardest task [he] ever undertook, in leaving 'the colony in great prosperity and peace, contrary to many men's expectations'. With him were John Rolfe, his wife Rebecca and their little son Thomas, as well as her entourage of about a dozen Indians and a cargo of Rolfe's tobacco. Pocahontas was of particular importance, brought over to show off 'the nonpareil of Virginia', to demonstrate the colonists' success in Christianising and civilising, and to boost the confidence of potential investors. After the party's slow coach journey up to London, the Company installed them in an inn in Ludgate Hill, variously known as the 'Belle Sauvage' or 'Bell Savage', after an old French romance of a beautiful woman discovered in a forest. Despite this somewhat facetious PR gesture, the Company allowed her and her people only £4 a week for maintenance.

Hearing of her arrival, Smith, though busy with his new book, presumed (according to his *Generall Historie*) to address a formal letter to Queen Anne, to make Pocahontas's 'qualities known to the Queen's most excellent Majesty and her court'. In this letter he provided the first written account of her rescue of him, how 'she hazarded the beating out of her own brains to save [his]', and then helped to save the colony from starvation. It was important that she be treated, not as a sideshow spectacle of the kind mentioned in *The Tempest*, nor as merely the wife of an ordinary gentleman, but as an Indian princess 'of so great a spirit, however her stature', who could be of great assistance in helping the English to 'rightly have a kingdom' in Virginia.

It appears that she was indeed introduced to the Queen at Court by Lady De La Warr, and attended several functions, including a performance in the Banqueting Hall of Ben Jonson's masque, *The Vision of Delight*, on 5 January 1617, a fantastic entertainment with singing, dancing, poetry, improbable drama, masked, grotesque entertainers and elaborate scenery, when the Queen danced with her husband's lover, the newly-created Earl of Buckingham. It is hard to imagine what the young woman from the Virginia woods made of it all. Others also treated with respect the daughter of a king; Samuel Purchas recalled that the Bishop of London 'entertained her with festival state and pomp beyond what I have seen in his great hospitality afforded to other ladies' (was the Bishop known for his kindness to ladies?). She also had her portrait painted, with an engraving by Simon van de Passe (at about the same time as his portrait of Smith), recording her true Indian name and giving her age as 27. She enjoyed her time in England.

Purchas spent more time with another Indian from her retinue, the priest Tomocomo, also known as Uttamatomakkin, discussing Indian religion ('devil-worship', thought Revd Purchas). This man had been sent by Powhatan to report on the English, with instructions to make a notch on a long stick for every Englishman he saw: 'he was quickly weary of that task,' and threw the stick away. Tomocomo also met Smith – perhaps to his surprise, having been told that Smith was dead (though Powhatan had doubted that). After catching up on recent events, he asked Smith about the English god and king. 'Concerning God, I told him the best I could,' recalled Smith, who told Tomocomo that he had already seen King James at Court. At first the Indian refused to believe that the shambling figure he had seen was indeed the King of England and Scotland. The royal manners had not impressed him either, contrasting Powhatan's – and Smith's – past diplomatic generosity with that of the King. 'You gave Powhatan a white dog, which Powhatan fed as himself, but your king gave me nothing, and I am better than your white dog.'

In all this time, Smith had not been to see Pocahontas – busyness in preparing for another American venture could be no excuse. At last, some time early in 1617, hearing that she was due soon to return to Virginia, he went to visit her, in the village of Brentford, to the west of London, near the Thames (and Richmond Palace). It was a tense meeting, long overdue, as they both knew. At first, she could not cope: 'after a modest salutation, without any word, she turned about, obscured her face, as not seeming well contented.' Met with her silence, Smith, Rolfe and the others present then left her for two or three hours, 'repenting myself,' he wrote, crassly, 'to have writ she could speak English.' When they met again, she reminded him of her past 'courtesies' – help – to him, and reproached him for his present manner to her: 'You did promise what was yours should be his

[Powhatan's], and he the like to you; you called him father, being in his land a stranger, and by the same reason so must I do you.'

Smith protested that he could not have her address him so, as she was a king's daughter (and – unsaid – here in England he was nobody special). 'With a well set countenance', she persisted, refusing his attempt to deny their past by setting English class barriers between them: 'Were you not afraid to come into my father's country, and caused fear in him and all his people (but me), and fear you here I should call you father? I tell you then I will, and you shall call me child, and so I will be for ever and ever your countryman.'

Another implicit reproach: 'They did tell us always you were dead, and I knew no other till I came to Plymouth' – months ago. 'Yet Powhatan did command Uttamatomakkin to seek you, and know the truth, because your countrymen will lie much.' In the past, he had been a man to be relied on; what was he now?

Whatever else they said, Smith did not record; and so they parted, for the last time – though linked together in the popular imagination, in her own words, 'for ever and ever'. In March 1617, she and her family set off to return to Virginia with Samuel Argall, but London, with its pestilences, contaminated water (Prince Henry had died of typhoid fever in 1612) and foul air had done for her. Already ill when she went aboard, she was taken ashore downriver at Gravesend, on the south bank of the Thames estuary, where she died and was buried on 21 March, in St George's graveyard. Purchas wrote, exercising the grim wit Jacobeans found appropriate for death, how 'she came at Gravesend to her end and grave, having given great demonstration of her Christian sincerity' – or of her native stoicism: as she lay dying, she told Rolfe, 'All must die; 'tis enough that the child liveth.'

The ship sailed on, but little Thomas was not well, and at Plymouth his father had him put ashore into the care of a local official, and never saw him again. Rolfe himself went on to Virginia, eventually remarried, and did well in the tobacco business (as did Thomas, after his father's death).

16

All That I Have

After the publication of *The Description of New England,* Smith worked hard to get another venture going, and eventually got a promise from the Plymouth Company to support a fleet of 20 ships for New England. The company's finances were as unreliable as ever, and when he got to Plymouth again, he found only three ships and a mere handful of prospective colonists. Settling for what he could get, however inadequate, he prepared to sail; but then a mighty south-west wind set in, keeping the little fleet trapped in harbour. When he had first set out for Virginia, the wind had kept him waiting off the Kent coast for over a month; now, the wind blew for three months. When at last it relented, it was too late to cross the Atlantic and set up a fort and plantation before the winter set in. The ships were sent off to do some fishing, to defray costs, and Smith went back to London, 'the quick forge and working-house of thought' (as the Chorus in *Henry V* put it).

Here he tried for a better class of supporter: he wrote a long letter to Sir Francis Bacon, who had replaced Salisbury as Lord Chancellor, in January 1618. This was in effect an extended business plan, presented to the great man with appropriate humility, providing not only a delicately angled view of recent history but indicating, in true salesman fashion, the rich potential for settlement in New England: no 'mines of gold', but secure bases manned by 'industrious subjects', fishing, fur trading, raw materials, timber for the navy. Five thousand pounds would be sufficient to set things up on a sound basis, without the rush for quick profits that had spoiled earlier ventures.

There was no reply. Nevertheless, it is clear that Bacon had learned from what Smith had to say, here and elsewhere, when he wrote his own essay, 'Of Plantations' (published 1625). In this, he agrees with Smith in not putting merchants in charge, who 'look ever to the present gain', or taking 'wicked condemned men to be the people ... for they will ever live like rogues and not fall to work ... and then certify over to their country to the discredit of the plantation'. Practical men should be taken, and plants appropriate to the soil, 'to defray the charge of the plantation; so it be not, as was said, hath fared with tobacco in Virginia'. The plantation should not be 'in marsh or unwholesome grounds', and the natives treated 'justly and graciously, but with sufficient guard nevertheless'.

Elsewhere, there was growing interest in colonisation in America. King James's toleration of religious nonconformists was never very great, and considerable numbers of the more extreme sects and rejectionists, known as Separatists, had gone abroad, particularly to the Netherlands, to practise their religion. From Amsterdam they went to Leiden, but still could not settle; fearing compromise and assimilation in this different culture, they resolved to find 'a world elsewhere'. After extended negotiations in 1619, the Virginia Company granted them a patent for land in the north of the Company's territory, near the mouth of the River Hudson. The Pilgrims, so-called, knew they would need assistance; however, they did not take the strong-willed, religiously orthodox Captain Smith as their guide, despite his offer to go with them and his unequalled experience of eastern north America and its natives. Instead, they took his maps and writings, and a Captain Miles Standish, another Netherlands wars veteran, without American or Atlantic experience. Bad weather and poor navigation took their ship, the *Mayflower*, off course, away from the Hudson towards Cape Cod and a place Prince Charles had named Plymouth (Smith's 'Accomac'), landing in November 1620. That was probably Smith's last chance.

Smith was not one to waste time or labour. Still resilient at the age of 40, despite his 11 years of frustration since he left Virginia, he replaced his sword with his pen. He revised and expanded his letter, and in December 1620 it was entered for publication under the title, *New Englands Trialls* (= ventures or attempts), with maps of both New England and Virginia, to be circulated among possible interested parties, especially city guilds and companies throughout England. His frustration is apparent: 'I never had power and means to do anything ... but in such penurious and miserable manner, as if I had gone a-begging to build a University; where[as] had men been as forward to adventure their purses as to crop the fruits of my labours, thousands ere this had been bettered by these designs. Thus betwixt the spur of desire and the bridle of reason I am near ridden to death in a ring of despair.' (The combination of spur and bridle seems like a memory of his riding lessons, but is actually a traditional emblem, depicting not frustration but the mature combination of controlled energy.) He even petitioned the Virginia Company for some reward for his efforts on their behalf; characteristically, the rich men gave him nothing.

Meanwhile, further south in Virginia, the colony had prospered, and expanded in both numbers and territory, with plantations scattered on both sides of the James River, in an area of some 140 square miles. The natives naturally viewed all this takeover of their land with increasing concern. Powhatan had died in 1618, and was succeeded briefly by his brother Opitchapam and then by Smith's old adversary, Opechancanough. The new chief changed his name, to Mangopeesomon; the colonists did not realise that this had any significance. In fact, it marked his intention for a different course of action, from apparently peaceable accommodation – he had even pretended to be interested in Christianity, and assured the Governor of his eagerness to keep the peace. Rather than cause trouble, he said, 'the sky should sooner fall'.

On the morning of 22 March 1622, the Indians suddenly attacked all the peaceful and unsuspecting English settlements, to which they now had ready and open access, slaughtering and maiming well over 300 men, women and children, between a third or a quarter of all the colonists. The hope was that, even if not all the invaders were killed, the shock would be such that the colony would be abandoned. The reaction was just the opposite: when news got back to England in July, the general demand was for vengeful slaughter and the extirpation of these inhuman barbarians, as they were generally regarded. Purchas wrote that 'Justice cryeth to God for vengeance, and in his name adjureth prudence and fortitude to the execution.' Christopher Brooke wrote, in *A Poem on the Late Massacre in Virginia*, of inhuman Indians:

> For, but consider what those creatures are,
> (I cannot call them men) no character
> Of God in them: souls drowned in flesh and blood;
> Rooted in evil, and opposed in good;
> Errors of nature, of inhuman birth,
> The very dregs, garbage and spawn of earth.

Therefore, he went on,

> What fear or pity were it, or what sin,
> (The rather since with us they thus begin),
> To 'quite their slaughter, leaving not a creature
> That may restore such shame of men and Nature?

Smith, while shocked, was less surprised than other people were: the colonists, he pointed out, had been complacent, not kept up their guard and allowed the natives free access to their settlements and use of their weapons. He had been 'amazed', he wrote, that the natives had been 'employed in hunting and fowling with our fowling pieces, and our men rooting in the ground about tobacco, like swine; besides, that the savages that do little but continually exercise their bow and arrows should dwell and lie so familiarly amongst our men that practised little but the spade.' His 1622 edition of *New Englands Trialls* emphasised his former ability in subduing the natives: 'When I had but ten men able to go forward ... I ranged that unknown country 14 weeks; I had but 18 to subdue them all, with which great army I stayed six weeks ... .' Now he proposed that he be sent out with a force of 100 soldiers and 30 sailors, not to exterminate, but 'by God's assistance ... [to] endeavour to enforce the savages to leave their country, or bring them in that fear and subjection that every man should follow their business securely.' However, the Company could not or would not fund such an expeditionary force, so it was left to the rearmed colonists to deal with the Indians themselves (which they did, ruthlessly), and for Smith to stay at home.

This edition of *New Englands Trialls* provided the first public mention of his rescue by Pocahontas. 'It is true in our greatest extremity they shot me, slew three of my men, and by the folly of them that fled took me prisoner [an unjust accusation: but when was Smith ever at fault?]; yet God made Pocahontas, the King's daughter, the means to deliver me.' Apart from indicating his military skills, he points out his foresight in anticipating the colony's future success in exporting furs and fish, the product of his own efforts. 'By that acquaintance I have with them [the American colonies] I may call them my children, for they have been my wife, my hawks, my hounds, my cards, my dice, and in total my best content.' The boast has its own pathos. Wifeless, childless, with no gentlemanly amusements, he was left with frustrated hopes and proud – and sometimes bitter – retrospection.

At some time that autumn, Smith went to Samuel Purchas, whose great travel compendium, *Purchas His Pilgrimes*, had been published that summer, to discuss another proposal, that would bear fruit as *The Generall Historie of Virginia, New-England, and the Summer Isles* (a title probably influenced by Richard Knolles's great *Generall Historie of the Turkes*, of 1603 and 1621, that Smith was bound to have looked at). This was not envisaged as the sort of objective analysis such as a modern historian might attempt. Rather, it was a collection of writings by Smith himself and several others, elaborated by quotations from various sources, to provide an account of events in Virginia – what was done, what was not done, what might have been done – from Smith's point of view: 'I am no compiler by hearsay, but have been a real actor … I have deeply hazarded myself in doing and suffering, and why should I stick to hazard my reputation in recording?' He might play up his own doings or diminish those of others, but he would not lie. He had a story to tell, and an objective to pursue: to stimulate others. As he wrote in a prospectus appealing for financial support and subscriptions: 'The story will give you satisfaction, and stir up a double new life in the adventurers, when they shall see plainly the causes of all those defailments and how they may be amended.'

Material came from his own experience and previous writings, from Hakluyt's and Purchas's collections, and from some contemporaries. He was also influenced by *A Relation of a Journey* (1615), by George Sandys, former Treasurer of the Virginia Colony, filled with quotations from and allusions to classical and foreign writers. Perhaps of more imme- diate influence was the *Atheomastix, The Scourge of Atheists* (1622), by Martin Fotherby, Bishop of Salisbury, which would have appealed to the soundly Protestant Smith. This work is decorated with quotations and translations from classical poets, which Smith in turn adopted and adapted, with varying degrees of appropriateness. The book, published by Michael Sparkes, of Eynsham, near Oxford, was to have maps of the Roanoke area, Virginia, New England and Bermuda (the Summer Isles), with several illustrations, notably of his patron, Frances, Countess of Hertford by her second marriage and Duchess of Richmond by her third (Smith's *A Map of Virginia* had been dedicated to her second husband). A former celebrated beauty, now the greatest lady in the country, enor- mously rich and recently widowed, she financed the book, allowed him to include a picture of her, and accepted his dedication, in which she appears as the latest in a series of helpful ladies (Tragabigzanda, Cal- lamata, Pocahontas and Madame Chanoyes), extending benevolence to their errant knight.

The book had 15 commendatory verses, including four by recent colo- nists. Most writers made play with Smith's name. So, T.T. writes how

From far fetched Indies and Virginia's soil,

Here Smith is come to show his art and skill:

He was the smith that hammered famine's foil,

And on Powhatan's Emperor had his will... .

Smith's present frustration is indicated:

This there he did and now is home returned,

To show us all that there did never go,

That in his heart he deeply oft hath mourned,

Because the action goeth on so slow ...

Samuel Purchas pulled out all his neo-classical stops, in stunningly over-compressed denunciation of Smith's opponents and commendation of his transformation from warrior to writer:

Lo here Smith's forge, where forgery's rogue-branded,

True Pegasus is shoed, fetters are forged

For silk-sots, milk-sops, base sloth, far hence landed

(Soil-changed*, soul-soiled still) England's dregs, discharged,

To plant (supplant) Virginia, home-disgorged:

Where Virtue's praise frames good men's stories' armour

'Gainst Time, Achilles-like, with best arts charged;

Pallas, all-armed, all-learned, can teach sword-grammar,

Can pens of pikes, arms t'arts, to scholar, soldier hammer ...

('Soil-changed' is annotated: *Coelum non animum mutant*, for those who changed their skies but not their natures.) Etcetera, etcetera.

Some of the verses lament Smith's lack of financial reward, and this becomes somewhat a recurrent undertone; in the prospectus, he wrote how 'these observations are all that I have for the experiences of a thousand pound, and the loss of eighteen years of time, besides the trials, dangers, miseries and encumbrances I have endured for my country's good gratis.' Likewise in the main work he notes that 'in neither of these two countries [Virginia and New England] have I one foot of land, nor the very house I builded, nor the ground I digged with my own hands, nor ever any content or satisfaction at all.' The last words seem to have a resonance going beyond complaints about land or money, to a sense, after a lifetime's expense of spirit, of the futility of endeavour, and empty dissatisfaction.

He was not the only one for whom things had not gone well. The Virginia Company had gone bankrupt, and in May 1623 a commission was set up to look into its condition. In Book IV of the *Generall Historie* Smith records his testimony to the commission, repeating his well-established views: it was essential to have the right kind of colonists, including hard-working, competent craftsmen and labourers, capable local leaders, and adequate numbers of soldiers for security. It would be better, he thought, for the Company to be replaced by royal control; in May 1624, the Virginia Company ceased to exist, and Virginia became a royal colony.

It appears that, at around this time, Smith showed Purchas a summary account of his Transylvanian experiences, which was included in *Purchas His Pilgrimes*. Purchas encouraged Smith to take the laisser-passer given him by Zsigmond Bathory, 'intimating the service he had done, and the honours he had received', to Sir William Segar, Garter King of Arms, who approved his coat of arms in August 1625.

Meanwhile, King James had died in March 1625, to be succeeded by his second son, Charles. Charles's sister, Elizabeth, had married a German prince, who became King of Bohemia, but had been deposed and driven out by the Catholic Austrians and Spanish in 1619. Charles now prepared for war; after James's long, pacific policy, a new army and navy would have to be equipped and trained. It was time, as Andrew Marvell wrote of a later conflict, 'to oil the unuse'd armour's rust'. Gervase Markham, a soldier, brought out a DIY manual, *The Soldiers' Accidence, or An Introduction into Military Discipline*, and Sir Henry Mainwaring, former privateer and now Deputy Warden of the Cinque

Ports, wrote *The Seaman's Dictionary*. Smith had plenty of experience at
sea; using that, and any other material he could lay hands on, in October
1626 he brought out the first English instruction manual for would-be
seamen. Its title – in shortened form – was: *An Accidence, or The Pathway
to Experience Necessary for all Young Seamen*. The author was described
as 'sometime Governor of Virginia, and Admiral of New England'. The
little book discusses the rudiments of naval equipment and practice,
with the naming of parts and detailing of duties, from master and mate
through gunner and cook, to swabber and liar: 'The liar is to hold his
place but for a week, and he that is first taken with a lie, every Monday
is so proclaimed at the mainmast by a general cry, "A liar, a liar, a liar";
he is under the swabber, and only to clean the beakhead and chains [the
heads, or privy]'.

Markham had followed up with a second book, *The Soldiers'
Grammar*, and in 1627 Smith likewise brought out *A Sea Grammar,
with the plain Exposition of Smith's Accidence for young Seamen enlarged*.
The dedication to the Lords and Privy Council introduces his (literary)
model: 'Julius Caesar wrote his own Commentaries, holding it no less
honour to write, than fight ... I have been a miserable practitioner in this
school of war by sea and land more than thirty years, however chance
or occasion have kept me from your lordships' knowledge or employment.' Among the seven commendatory verses, John Hagthorpe help-
fully remarks,

> If merit and desert were truly weighed
> In Justice scales, not all by money swayed,
> Smith should not want reward, with many mo[r]e,
> Whom sad oblivion now doth overflow.

The book amplifies material from *An Accidence* and Mainwaring, with
instructions on shipbuilding from the keel up, and names of everything
from 'puttocks' and 'cat harpings' to 'leech lines' and 'drabblers', as well
as the language and instruction for putting to sea, responding to various

winds and storm conditions, and notes on different kinds of ordnance, from roundshot, crossbar shot and trundle shot to grenades (very like the firepots or Greek fire he had used against the Turks years ago). Particularly notable is a bravura paragraph, expanded from the previous book, and based to a considerable extent, it seems probable, on personal experience, on the method of attacking another ship. Composed largely in dialogue form, it seems worth quoting fairly fully (with added punctuation):

'A sail!' 'How stands she, to windward or leeward?' Set him by the compass. He stands right ahead (or on the weather bow, or lee bow); but fly your colours (if you have a consort, or else not). Out with all your sails, a steady man to the helm. 'Sit close, to keep her steady.' Give chase or fetch him up. 'He holds his own, no, we gather on him; out goes his flag and ... top armings ... .' 'Captain, he furls and slings his mainsail, in goes his spritsail.' Thus they use to strip themselves unto their short sails, or fighting sails ... . 'Master, how stands the chase?' 'Right on head, I say.' 'Well, we shall reach him by and by. What, is all ready?' 'Yea, yea.' Every man to his charge, dowse your topsail, to salute him for the sea. Hail him with a noise of trumpets. 'Whence is your ship?' 'Of Spain, whence is yours?' 'Of England.' 'Are you merchants or men of war?' 'We are of the sea.' He waves us to leeward, with his drawn sword calls amain for the King of Spain, and springs his luff [heads closer to windward]. Give him a chase piece with your broadside, and run ahead a good berth of him. 'We have the wind of him.' As he tacks about, tack you about also and keep your luff. Be yare at the helm, edge in with him, give him a volley of small shot, also your prow and broadside as before, and keep your luff. 'He pays us shot for shot.' 'Well, we shall requite him. What, are you ready again?' 'Yea, yea.' 'Try him once more, as before.' 'Done, done.' Keep your luff and load your ordnance again. 'Is all ready?' 'Yea, yea.' Edge in with him again, begin with your bow pieces, proceed with your broadside, and bring her round that the stern may also discharge, and your tacks close aboard again. 'Done, done. The wind veers, the sea goes too high to board her, and we are shot through and through, and between wind and water.' Try the pump, bear up the helm. 'Master, let us breathe and refresh a little, and sling a man overboard to stop the leaks.' That is, to truss him up about the middle in a piece of canvas, and a rope to keep him from sinking and his arms at liberty, with a mallet in the one hand and a plug lapped in oakum and well tarred in a tarpaulin clout in the other, which he will quickly beat into the hole or holes the bullets made. 'What cheer, mates, is all well?' 'All well, all well, all well.' [The battle is broken off, the ships separate, the wounded and dead are seen to, everything made good.] 'Boy!' 'Holla, master!' 'Holla! Is the kettle boiled?' 'Yea, yea.' 'Boatswain, call up the men to prayer and breakfast.'

Meanwhile, in September, 1626, his old friend and mentor, the Revd Samuel Purchas, had died, aged 48 – a reminder of mortality for the 46-year old Smith. At some time in the next couple of years he was approached by the noted scholar and antiquarian, Sir Robert Bruce Cotton, who had read the *Generall Historie*, and been impressed by what it revealed of its author. Now he urged Smith to write his own story. (He would not have used the word 'autobiography': the OED gives its earliest appearance in print as 1809.)

This was Smith's cue, like Othello's, to tell his heroic story,

> of most disastrous chances,
> Of moving accidents by flood and field,
> Of hair-breadth 'scapes i'th'imminent deadly breach,
> Of being taken by the insolent foe,
> And sold to slavery, of [his] redemption thence,
> And portance in [his] travel's history ...

The story could not fail to 'give satisfaction', to use his phrase, but the book itself is oddly frustrating in its execution. The title, *The True Travels, Adventures, and Observations of Captain John Smith, in Europe, Asia, Africa, and America from Anno Domini 1593 to 1629*, suggests that it might be one of the travel books becoming popular at the time, except that he provides little by way of travelogue or descriptions of foreign parts. Neither does he provide much self-revelation. Part of the problem was that he had no real models to work from. People in general did not write autobiographies disclosing their private lives, thoughts and feelings (he is unlikely to have known the self-exploratory essays of Montaigne, even though they had been translated by John Florio in 1603). His model, insofar as he had one, was one he had had to study at school: Julius Caesar. In the *Generall Historie* he had written, 'Where shall we find a Julius Caesar, whose achievement shone as clear in his own Commentaries, as they did in the field?'

Now he wrote, like Caesar, in the third person, not of his thoughts but of his actions; never does he tell us of fear, hope or excitement, rather, of what he or someone else did, or did next. Did he have a love – or even a sex – life? He does not let us know; most of his earlier life was spent in all-male communities, though he romanticised various mostly inaccessible women, in accordance with his knight-errant self-image. What about religion, far more important then to most people than nowadays? All we know is that he was rather conventionally pious, and noticeably proper. One of his fellow-soldiers, Thomas Carlton, wrote of him, 'I never knew a warrior yet, but thee / From wine, tobacco, debts, dice, oaths, so free.' He was ambitious and patriotic, outspoken and with an edge to his tongue, with a sense of honour, underlaid by respect for hard work and disrespect for arrogance.

After a couple of curiously muddled pages about his youth (embarrassment about his modest origins, unacknowledged hostility to his parents, sheer impatience?), vagueness about his time in the Netherlands (presumably as an undistinguished ranker – a modern writer would have made much of the first experience of muddy, bloody warfare), and a lively account of the sea-fight in the Straits of Otranto, he reproduces most of the material already printed in Purchas's *Pilgrimes*; a little padding and borrowing here and there, and the job – 60 folio pages – was done. Once again there were commendatory verses, and some entertaining illustrations. One Master Hawkins came up with a good phrase – 'Thou

that hast had a spirit to fly like thunder' – and defended Smith from his
detractors:

> For none can truly say thou didst deceive
> Thy soldiers, sailors, merchants nor thy friends,
> But all from thee a true account receive,
> Yet nought to thee all these thy virtues brings.

A final chapter, bizarrely and irrelevantly, provides an account of English
piracy over the previous half-century, denouncing piracy and urging
sailors to – his established obsession – 'adventure to those fair plantations of our English nation': colonisation, and a new England.

The few pages remaining here indicate we are coming towards the end.
March 1631 sees his last appeal for energetic commitment to colonialisa-
tion. He called it, *Advertisements for the unexperienced Planters of New
England, or anywhere*. He begins by expressing his pleasure in the new
colonies: 'Pardon me if I offend in loving that I have cherished truly by the
loss of my prime fortunes, means and youth, if it overglad me to see industry herself adventure now to make use of my aged endeavours.' Whilst the
book as a whole celebrates and encourages colonial endeavours to make a
new and better England overseas, the first chapters nevertheless contain
familiar criticisms of the original Virginia Company, for sending out 'so
many refiners, goldsmiths, jewellers ... spies and superintendents' as well as
troublesome 'roarers' and 'loiterers', with insufficient useful working-men;
particular criticism is reserved for his old bugbear, burdensome, non-pro-
ductive gentlemen, such as 'Lord Delaware for Governor, with as many
great and stately offices under him as doth belong to a great kingdom, with
good sums for their extraordinary expenses.' Smith was part of the under-
current of class resentment, not necessarily or consciously radical, that
was to contribute to the great tsunami of the Civil War, only 11 years away.
He disapproves of 'Brownists, Anabaptists, Papists, Puritans, Separatists'
as colonists, in favour of mainstream 'good Catholic Protestants', who are
prepared to work, and work together. He points out that there should be

enough land for all workers, as European infections are clearing the way: 'It seems God hath provided this country for our nation, destroying the natives by the plague, it not touching one Englishman.'

Briefly he reviews his own career, that has brought him to this. 'Having lived near 37 years [1595 to 1631, inclusive] in the midst of wars, pestilence and famine, by which many an hundred thousand have died about me, and scarce five living of them went first with me to Virginia, and [now to] see the fruits of my labours thus well begin to prosper; though I have but my labour for my pains, have I not much reason both privately and publicly to acknowledge it and give God thanks ... .' Building a colony, he admits, 'is not a work for everyone ... it requires all the best parts of art, judgement, courage, honesty, constancy, diligence and industry, to do near well.' He urges the colonists to imitate those 'brave spirits that advanced themselves from poor soldiers to great Captains'. 'John Smith writ this with his own hand,' is appended to the book.

Curiously, on the back of the dedicatory page, is a poem, unsigned, not a commendatory verse. Some think it is by Smith, though it seems technically rather accomplished (Sir Francis Bacon used the verse form in a poem published in 1630). It might derive from meetings connected with *An Accidence*, a few years earlier, that included in its dedication the Masters and Wardens of Trinity House, responsible for all sea marks, such as beacons and buoys. The inclusion of this poem, about a warning buoy on a wreck, suggests a weariness of spirit in John Smith, as his 51st birthday approached (as with old cars, it is not the age that matters, it is the mileage – and, with Smith, battered in body and spirit, there had been a lot of mileage).

The Sea Mark

Aloof, aloof; and come not near,
    the dangers do appear;
Which if my ruin had not been
    you had not seen.
I only lie upon the shelf

to be a mark to all
　　which on the same might fall,
　　That none may perish but myself.
If in or outward you be bound,
　　do not forget to sound;
Neglect of that was cause of this
to steer amiss.
The seas were calm, the wind was fair,
that made me so secure, [complacent]
that now I must endure
All weathers, be they foul or fair.

The winter's cold, the summer's heat
　　alternatively beat
Upon my bruisèd sides, that rue
　　because too true
That no relief can ever come.
But why should I despair
　　being promisèd so fair
That there shall be a day of Doom. [Judgement]

A month later, John Smith was dying. The cause is unknown; there
was plague in London, as so often, but he had time to make his will, but
signing only with a cross, on 21 June, 1631, when he died. To Thomas
Parker, one of the King's Privy Seal clerks, he left his Lincolnshire property and his grant of arms, and a share in his library with John Tradescant,
gardener to the King and collector of curiosities (including 'Powhatan's
mantle', now in the Ashmolean Museum, Oxford). His brother's widow
and a 'Mistris Tredway' received small bequests. He left £20 for his
funeral expenses. There was not much to leave.

John Smith was buried in St Sepulchre's Church, in London. An
anonymous friend arranged for him to have a memorial tablet:

To the living memory of his deceased friend
Captain John Smith,
sometime Governor of Virginia,
and Admiral of New England,
who departed this life the 21st of June 1631.
ACCORDAMUS VINCERE EST VIVERE

It begins with an acknowledgement of his almost incredible achievements –

Here lies one that hath conquered Kings,
Subdued large teritories, and done things
Which to the world impossible would seem,
But that the truth is held in more esteem... .

It reviews his conquests of the Turks and the Powhatans, and establishment of the colony in Virginia. It concludes,

But what avails his conquests, now he lies
Interred in earth, a prey to worms and flies?
O! May his soul in sweet Elysium sleep,
Until the Keeper that all souls doth keep
Return to Judgement; and that, after thence,
With angels he may have his recompense.

There seems to be a pun in the last line: in his lifetime, Smith got very little recompense in the form of gold angels (coins) – it would have to be after his death that he got the recognition he deserved.

In *True Travels,* Smith, classically-educated Elizabethan to the core, wrote, 'Seeing honour is our lives' ambition, and our ambition after death, to have an honourable memory of our life; and seeing by no means we would be abated of the dignity and glory of our predecessors, let us imitate their virtues to be worthily their successors.' People do not seem to think like that, nowadays; but Smith did – and did pretty well.

References and Further Reading

Anyone who writes on Captain John Smith is indebted to the exhaustive research of Philip L Barbour, in *The Three Worlds of Captain John Smith* (Houghton Mifflin, Boston, and Macmillan, London: 1964, and his edition of *The Complete Works of Captain John Smith* (3 vol.) (University of North Carolina Press, Chapel Hill, and London: 1986). All quotations from Smith are from this edition:

Vol. I: *A True Relation*, 1608, *A Map of Virginia* and *The Proceedings of the English Colony*, 1612, *A Description of New England*, 1616, Letter to Sir Francis Bacon, 1618, *New Englands Trials*, 1622.
Vol. II: *The General History of Virginia*, 1623, 1624.
Vol. III: *An Accidence or The Pathway to Experience*, 1626, *A Sea Grammar*, 1627, *The True Travels, Adventures and Observations of Captain John Smith*, 1630, *Advertisements for the Unexperienced ...*, 1631, and fragments and auxiliary documents, including the wills of George and John Smith, and John Smith's epitaph.

Chapter 1: Upon Brave Adventures
Brinsley, John, *Ludus Literarius, or the Grammar* School (London: 1612).

Charlton, K, *Education in Renaissance England* (Routledge, London: 1965).

Harrison, William, *A Description of England* (London: 1587).

Lithgow, William, *The totall discourse of the rare adventures* (1614, 1623, repr. MacLehose, Glasgow: 1906), hereafter Lithgow, *The totall discourse*.

Pooley, Roger (ed.), *George Gascoigne. The Green Knight* (Carcanet, Manchester: 1982).

Smith, John, *The True Travels*.

Temple, Sir Richard Carnac (ed.), *The Travels of Peter Mundy, 1608–1667* (1668; 5 vol. Hakluyt Soc., Cambridge: 1907–36).

West, Jane, *The Brave Lord Willoughby. An Elizabethan Soldier* (Pentland, Edinburgh: 1998).

Chapter 2: To Conquer is to Live

Herford, C H, and P & E Simpson (eds.), *The Works of Ben Jonson* (11 vol.) (Oxford University Press: 1925–52), hereafter Herford et al. (eds.), *Works of Ben Jonson*.

Jorgensen, Christer, et al., *Fighting Techniques of the Modern World, 1500–1763* (Spellmount, Staplehurst: 2005).

Lithgow, *The totall discourse*.

Murphey, Rhoads, *Ottoman Warfare, 1500–1700* (University College London Press, London: 1999).

Riggs, David, *Ben Jonson. A Life* (Harvard University Press, Cambridge, Mass., and London: 1989).

Smith, Bradford, *Captain John Smith, His Life and Legend* (with appendix by Polanyi Striker) (Lippincott, Philadelphia: 1953).

Smith, John, *The True Travels*.

Chapter 3: Dangerous Service

Hughes, Charles (ed.), *Shakespeare's Europe. Unpublished Chapters of Fynes Moryson's Itinerary* (Sherratt & Hughes, London: 1903).

Purchas, Samuel, *Hakluytus Posthumus, or Purchas His Pilgrimes* (5 vol.) (1625, repr. 20 vol., MacLehose, Glasgow: 1905–07), hereafter Purchas, *Purchas His Pilgrimes*.

Sandys, George, *A Relation of a Journey* (1615).

Smith, John, *The True Travels* and *A Sea Grammar*.

Chapter 4: Go West, Young Man

Barbour, Philip L (ed.), *The Jamestown Voyages Under the First Charter, 1606–1609* (2 vol.) (Hakluyt Society, Cambridge: 1969) (includes Archer, Newport, Percy, Todkill, Wingfield.), hereafter Barbour (ed.), *The Jamestown Voyages*.

Buxton, John (ed.), *Michael Drayton: Poems* (2 vol.) (Routledge, London: 1953).

Chisney, David Bair, *Sir Humphrey Gilbert, Elizabeth's Racketeer* (Harper, N.Y.: 1932).

Dick, Oliver Lawson (ed.), *Aubrey's Brief Lives* (Secker & Warburg, London: 1949).

Elliott, J H, *Empires of the Atlantic World. Britain and Spain in America, 1492–1830* (Yale University Press, New Haven and London: 2006).

Gray, Robert, *A Good Speed to Virginia* (1609, repr. Scholars' Facsimiles and Reprints, N.Y.: 1937), hereafter Gray, *A Good Speed to Virginia*; and see Alexander Brown, *The Genesis of the United States* (Russell & Russell, N.Y.: 1964).

Hakluyt, Richard, *The Principall Navigations, Voiages, Trafiques and Discoveries of the English Nation* (1589, repr. 12 vol., Hakluyt Society, Cambridge: 1903–05).

Herford et al. (eds.), *Works of Ben Jonson*.

Quinn, David B (ed.), *The Roanoke Voyages, 1584–1590* (2 vol.) (Hakluyt Society, Cambridge: 1955).

———, *England and the Discovery of America, 1541–1621* (Knopf, N.Y.: 1974).

Chapter 5: Getting To Know You

Barbour, Philip L, *Pocahontas and her World* (Robert Hale, London: 1971).

——(ed.), *The Jamestown Voyages*.

Percy, George, *A Trewe Relatyon of the Proceedinges and Occurences of Moment* (1613), hereafter Percy, *A Trewe Relatyon* (and see Barbour (ed.), *The Jamestown Voyages*).

Rountree, Helen C, *Pocahontas's People. The Powhatan Indians of Virginia through Four Centuries* (University of Oklahoma Press, Norman and London: 1990).

Smith, John, *The General History, Advertisements*.

Strachey, William, *The historie of travell into Virginia Britannia* (1612; repr ed. Louis B Wright, Hakluyt Society, Cambridge: 1953), hereafter Strachey, *The historie of travell*.

——, 'A True Reportory of the Wreck and Redemption of Sir Thomas Gates, Knight,' in Louis B Wright (ed.), *A Voyage to Virginia in 1609* (University Press of Virginia, Charlottesville, Va.: 1964).

Chapter 6: Tuftataffety Humourists

Barbour (ed.), *The Jamestown Voyages*.

Smith, John, *The General History*.

Wingfield, Jocelyn R, *Virginia's True Founder: Edward-Maria Wingfield and His Times, 1550-c.1614* (Wingfield Family Soc., Athens, Ga.: 1993).

Chapter 7: Time of Trial

Adams, Henry, *The Education of Henry Adams: An Autobiography* (Houghton Mifflin, Boston: 1961).

Barbour (ed.), *The Jamestown Voyages*.

Smith, John, *The General History* and *The True Travels*.

Tilton, Robert S, *Pocahontas: The Evolution of an American Narrative* (Cambridge University Press, Cambridge, Mass., and Cambridge: 1994).

Chapter 8: Gilded Dirt

Barbour (ed.), *The Jamestown Voyages.*
Smith, John, *A Map of Virginia, The General History, The True Travels.*
Strachey, *The historie of travel.*
Symonds, William, *The Proceedings of the English Colony* in Barbour (ed.), *Complete Works of Captain John Smith*, Vol. I, hereafter Symonds, *Proceedings.*

Chapter 9: The Phoenix and the Nonpareil

Percy, George, *A Trewe Relatyon*, and see Purchas, *Purchas His Pilgrimes*, especially vols 18 and 19.
Smith, John, *The General History.*

Chapter 10: Trips Round the Bay

Gray, *A Good Speed to Virginia.*
Smith, John, *The General History.*
Symonds, *Proceedings.*

Chapter 11: Love You Not Me?

Smith, John, *The General History*
Symonds, *Proceedings.*

Chapter 12: There Comes Captain Smith

Purchas, *Purchas His Pilgrimes.*
Smith, John, *The General History.*
Strachey, *The historie of travel.*

Chapter 13: Things Fall Apart

Gray, *A Good Speed to Virginia.*

Smith, John, *The General History*.
Symonds, *Proceedings*.

Chapter 14: Since You've Been Gone
Fausz, Frederick, 'Patterns of Anglo-Indian Aggression' in Fitzhugh, W
W (ed.), *Cultures in Contact* (Smithsonian Inst. Press, Washington
and London: 1985)
Hamor, Ralph, *A True Discourse of the Present State of Virginia* (1616,
repr. Da Capo Press, Amsterdam and N.Y.:1971).
Land, Robert Hunt, 'Henrico and Its College', *William and Mary
Quarterly*, Ser.2, Vol.18 (1938), pp 453–98.
Percy, *A Trewe Relatyon*.
Price, David A, *Love and Hate in Jamestown* (Knopf, N.Y.: 2003; Faber
& Faber, London: 2004).
Purchas, *Purchas His Pilgrimes*.

Chapter 15: Perplexed Thoughts
Smith, John, *Description of New England, New Englands Trials, The
General History, Advertisements*.
Strachey, *The historie of travel*.

Chapter 16: All That I Have
Bacon, Francis, *Essayes* (1625, repr., Everyman, London: 1915).
———, Poem in Sylvester, Joshua, *Panthea, or Divine Wishes* (1630).
Fotherby, Martin, *Atheomastix. The Scourge of Atheists* (1622).
Grosart, A B (ed.), *Christopher Brooke. The Complete Poems* (Fuller's
Worthies, London: 1872).
Kingsbury, Susan Myra (ed.), *The Records of the Virginia Company of
London*, (4 vol.) (US Govt. Printing Office, Washington D.C.:
1906–35).
Sandys, George, *A Relation of a Journey* (1615).
Smith, John, *New Englands Trials, The General History, Accidence, A
Sea Grammar, The True Travels, Advertisements*.

Picture Sources

The author and publishers wish to express their thanks to the following sources of illustrative material and/or permission to reproduce it.

Akg Images London, The Bridgeman Art Library, The British Museum, The Codrington Library, All Soul's College, Oxford. Corbis, Getty Images, Topham Picturepoint

Index